We Shall Return
Women of Palestine

Ingela Bendt and James Downing

Translated by Ann Henning

Zed Press Ltd, 57 Caledonian Road, London N1 9DN, UK

Lawrence Hill and Co., 520 Riverside Avenue, Westport, Conn. 06880, USA

We Shall Return was originally published in Swedish by Prisma Bokforlaget, and in English jointly by Zed Press Ltd., 57 Caledonian Road, London N1 9DN and Lawrence Hill and Co., 520 Riverside Avenue, Westport, Conn. 06880 in 1982.

Copyright © Ingela Bendt and James Downing, 1980
Translation Copyright © Zed Press, 1982

Copyedited by Irene Staunton and Beverley Brown
Proofread by Rosamund Howe
Cover design by Jan Brown
Cover photo by Ingela Bendt
Photographs in text by Ingela Bendt and James Downing
3 historical photos courtesy of PLO Cultural Arts Section
Map by Roy Bäckbom
Typeset by Margaret Cole
Printed by Krips Repro, Meppel, Holland

British Library Cataloguing in Publication Data

Bendt, Ingela
We shall return.
1. Palestinian Arabs — Lebanon 2. Refugees
I. Title   II. Downing Jim
III. Vi ska tilbaka till var jord. *English*
305.8'9275694'05692   DS86
ISBN 0-86232-042-9
ISBN 0-86232-087-9 Pbk

USA ISBN: 0 88208 154 3
           0 88208 155 1 Pbk

Contents

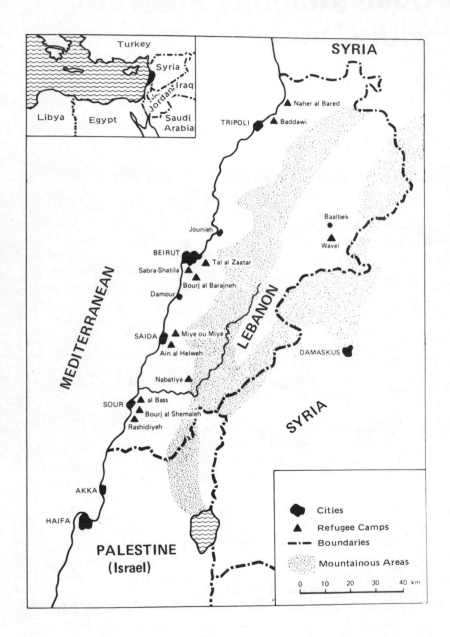

Turkey

Syria

Libya Egypt Iraq
Jordan
Saudi
Arabia

SYRIA

Naher al Bared

TRIPOLI Baddawi

Baalbek

Jounieh

BEIRUT

Sabra-Shatila Tal al Zaatar

Bourj al Barajneh

Damour

LEBANON

Wavel

DAMASKUS

SAIDA Miye ou Miye

Ain al Helweh

Nabatiya

SOUR al Bass

Bourj al Shemaleh

Rashidiyeh

SYRIA

MEDITERRANEAN

AKKA

HAIFA

PALESTINE
(Israel)

Cities

Refugee Camps

Boundaries

Mountainous Areas

0   10   20   30   40 km

Israel's War on the Lebanon: 'Like Shooting Sparrows with Cannons'

On Friday, Rashidiyeh was a fully functioning camp. By Monday, it had become a field of rubble.

The young Swedish nurse lowers her head and closes her eyes as if she were trying to blot out the memory of what happened that first weekend in June 1982 when Israel launched its invasion of Lebanon. Up until then, she had worked at the Palestinian Red Crescent Society clinic in Rashidiyeh, a Palestinian refugee camp in Southern Lebanon, 1 1/2 miles from the coastal city of Tyre.

This book is largely about Rashidiyeh. The camp no longer exists. Rashidiyeh was the first victim of the Israeli invasion. For two days, the 9,000 people living there, including the women you will meet in this book, huddled in underground shelters as the camp was subjected to almost constant shelling, helicopter attacks and massive air raids.

Outnumbered and outgunned, the camp militia finally fled after putting up a fierce resistance. On the morning of the third day, the population left their shelters. Carrying white flags and pleading for mercy, they approached the Israeli forces who had entered the camp the night before and occupied the school compound.

All males between the ages of 14 and 70 were separated from their families. Blindfolded and with their hands tied behind their backs, they were taken away to special POW camps further south and in Israel. The women and children of Rashidiyeh were herded together on the beaches and in the citrus groves outside the camp and forced to watch helplessly as the Israelis systematically destroyed what was left of their homes.

Rashidiyeh was only the beginning. Even as the camp was being reduced to rubble, the Israeli war machine struck on northwards. Everywhere, the story was the same.

The coastal cities of Tyre and Sidon were shaken by massive Israeli ground, sea and air attacks. When the invaders finally entered Tyre, less than half of its buildings were left standing and the population had fled. In Sidon, more than 1,500 people were killed and another 3,000 wounded during three days of intensive bombardment.

Most of the Palestinian refugee camps in Southern Lebanon were literally wiped off the map. The largest of them, Ain el Helweh, on the outskirts of Sidon, was pounded mercilessly. No one knows for sure how many people perished there, but eyewitnesses recount that the bodies of 500 women and children were found in a shelter that had received several direct hits. As in earlier attacks in the Tyre area, American-made cluster bombs were dropped on the camp.

The number of wounded was staggering. Overburdened with casualties and with most of their medical staff missing, doctors at the Ain el Helweh Hospital had to perform amputations without being able to provide their patients with any anaesthetics. Meanwhile Israeli troops were busy setting up headquarters a stone's throw away.

Everywhere, the destruction was massive and indiscriminate. Numerous Lebanese villages were demolished by advancing Israeli artillery units and tanks.

Neutral observers were stunned. As one exhausted UN officer remarked during the third week of the invasion: 'It was like shooting sparrows with cannons.'

As we write these lines, West Beirut has been in a state of siege for more than two weeks. Large portions of the city have been heavily shelled, not to mention the Palestinian refugee camps on the southern outskirts. Israeli forces have cut off water and electricity supplies. They have also sealed off the city, allowing no one to leave. Under the constant threat of a final Israeli assault on the city, the civilian population of close to 600,000 people have no alternative but to wait and pray that negotiations between the Lebanese Government, the PLO, Israel and the United States will avert a bloodbath.

Meanwhile, the whole of Southern Lebanon has been transformed into a huge refugee camp. 500,000 people are homeless, 10,000 have been killed and tens of thousands have been wounded. With no place to escape to, the civilian population has sought refuge under trees, on the beaches, and in blown-out and abandoned buildings.

ii

United Nations and International Red Cross aid shipments and personnel, initially turned away by the Israelis, have finally been allowed into the area. Their reports are harrowing. Olof Rydbeck, the head of UNRWA (the UN special agency for Palestinian refugees), summed up the devastation by saying that 'we're now back to where we began in Lebanon 32 years ago.'

The advancing Israeli Army has also separated Palestinians from Lebanese, distinguishing between the two by painting white crosses on the backs of Palestinian refugees. At least 6,000 Palestinian males over the age of 14 have been herded off to hastily set-up interrogation camps. Many of the prisoners have been beaten with nail-studded sticks and plastic ropes. Several eyewitnesses report incidents of direct torture. The less fortunate have been summarily executed upon capture.

Journalists who have been able to visit Southern Lebanon report that Palestinian refugee children there now play a new game. Here in the West it is known as 'Blind Man's Bluff'. The Palestinian children call it 'Survival'.

Another reporter tells of standing outside the ruins of the Rashidiyeh camp watching a group of Palestinian children playing on the beach as their parents rummage through the ruins in search of their personal belongings. As he stood there, he was approached by an old Palestinian man dressed in traditional clothing. The old man pointed towards the children and nodded.

'You see,' he said. 'There's our new leadership.'

Ingela Bendt and Jim Downing
July 1982

Preface

This book will deal mainly with women in Palestinian refugee camps. Many of them experienced the exodus of 1948 (see the Chronology at the end of this book); others were born in exile. Like the men, they are all yearning to return to their homes. We chose to write about the women because, so far, very little has been written about them.

We spent five months in Lebanon gathering material. Most of that time was spent living in Palestinian refugee camps where we talked to lots of women. In accordance with the wishes of many of them, however, the names used in the book are mainly fictitious.

Both of us have been familiar with the Middle East for a long time. Jim Downing, a Swedish American, grew up very near Arab settlements, Palestinian refugee camps, in the context of the Middle East crisis and the wars in the Lebanon. Jim lived in Beirut for twelve years, until 1968, and he has been back many times since then. He is a former Chairman of the Swedish Palestine groups. In his work he has constantly come up against the fact of how few people know about the Palestinians' plight. Hence this book.

Ingela Bendt, a freelance journalist, has visited Israel in the past and worked on a kibbutz in Galilee. Her first visit to Lebanon was in the spring of 1978 when she stayed with a Palestinian refugee family in a Beirut camp. That year she also received a journalistic scholarship from SIDA, the Swedish International Development Authority, to investigate the role of Palestinian women in the Palestinian liberation struggle.

We would like to thank all the hospitable people who, time and again, opened their homes and gave us food and beds; and all the people who gave us insight into the depth of human suffering and

1

We Shall Return!

the incredible strength of human endurance. We respect and support their struggle for a country of their own.

Ingela Bendt and Jim Downing
Stockholm, 1981.

1. 'Only the Women? What about the Others?'

Once you're over the top of the mountains on the road from Damascus and have proceeded down towards the Lebanese coast, it shouldn't be long before Beirut appears as a white sugar-loaf on the headland in the Mediterranean. But today we can't see Beirut. There is only a grey haze, a lot of traffic and a queue which crawls down, around bends and past villages clinging to the mountainsides. As we get closer to Beirut, the traffic is increasingly stopped by Syrian military vehicles, and we see Syrian soldiers entrenched behind sandbags on balconies and on road bends. The valley down towards Beirut is filled with a thick sunny haze.

After two weeks of driving from Sweden we are now approaching our goal. Then, suddenly, there is a loud bang above us — we're uncertain for another second — then there is another explosion, and yet another! Then all hell breaks loose! We see villages burning in the mountains to the north. What we had first thought was a sunny haze is grey smoke from burning trees and houses. From the next bend we see an enormous cloud, like that of a nuclear bomb, emerging from the Beirut harbour. A terrifying cloud of heavy, oily, impenetrable smoke, filling half the sky, coloured pink by the sun at the edges.

East Beirut and the mountains to the north are burning. There is a thunder of falling grenades, cannon fire and automatic machine gun fire; explosions roar among the mountains, filling every inch of the air. The noise is deafening.

Groups of people are standing at the roadside watching the clouds of smoke below. Syrian artillery has hit one of the oil tanks in the port of Beirut, and thousands of gallons of oil are in flames.

Now, in October 1978, fighting is raging between right-wing

3

Lebanese forces and the Syrians in the right-wing stronghold
in Beirut. We have walked straight into the worst fighting
Beirut has seen since the beginning of the Civil War in
Lebanon in 1975. A civil war in which over 60,000 out of
Lebanon's 4 million inhabitants have lost their lives.

*Underneath the mountains, hidden by the smoke of burning oil and the haze
of war, lie Beirut and the Mediterranean.*

The Western press usually refers to this war as a religious war
between the Christian and the Muslim populations in the country.
But the Lebanese War has nothing to do with religion. In very
simplified terms, it is a fight between rich and poor, right and
left, where the Israelis have linked up with the right and the
Palestinians with the left. In 1976, 30,000 Syrian soldiers moved
in on the side of the right wing in an attempt to stop the fighting.
But when the right continued its collaboration with Syria's enemy,
Israel, the Syrians turned their weapons against them.

We stop in the mountains above Beirut, in the village of Souk al

Gharb where the PLO — Palestine Liberation Organization — has
a boarding school for 450 Palestinian and martyred Lebanese
children, children who have lost one or both parents in the war.
   'Ahlan wa sahlan!' — Welcome to Lebanon! the headmaster
says, making a helpless gesture with his arms as the window-
panes rattle with the explosions. 'We Palestinians have nothing to
do with the fighting this time, but the odd grenade will still fall
on our refugee camps in Beirut. Here at the school we're fully
prepared. Another school some miles away was hit earlier on
today. You certainly haven't chosen the right time to come here!'
   He says this calmly and without irony. We're sitting in the
semi-darkness of a flickering candle. The electricity has gone,
Beirut and the mountains are covered in darkness. We see cascades
of fire, streamers of sparks crossing each other down in the streets
of East Beirut. A rocket flare slowly fades after lighting up large
areas of the city. A second later, the right wing — or the Syrians
— move forward. This goes on throughout the night and for
another four days.
   It feels unreal to be standing on the terrace looking down on
a live picture of war, a spectacle where we know that houses are
destroyed and people shot dead. We wonder whether we will get
used to this?
   We explain to the headmaster that we have come to Lebanon
mainly to learn about the Palestinian women's experience of the
War, their fight for liberation. . . . But he interrupts us with an
irritated gesture. 'Only the women? Why? What about the others?
You will deal with our problem *as a whole,* won't you?'
   The headmaster's reaction was only the first of many similar
reactions from both men and women. Why give the women special
treatment? it was asked, and we were met by uncomprehending,
indulgent smiles: 'For you, in the West, women's circumstances
are a luxury to investigate, here we're fighting for our lives!' But
we were also to come across a reaction of sincere astonishment,
above all from the women of the Palestine Women's Association:
'Really, it's about time, too! Strong traditions are keeping the
women down, although we are the ones to make the greatest
sacrifices. All the time we are the ones who sacrifice and suffer
the most. . . .' 'The woman carries two-thirds of the social responsibility, the man carries the rest.' Those were the exact words
of a young Palestinian we met.

A few days later, we were to leave the PLO school in Souk al
Gharb and proceed towards West Beirut, which was almost un-
touched by the continuing fighting. Right across the city there is
a barricaded border-line. On the east where the right wing resides,
war is raging, whilst on the west the home of the left and the
Palestinians, people try to live normally.

Before the Civil War, Beirut was the Monaco and Lichtenstein
of the Middle East. This is where Arab oil sheiks would meet the
representatives of Western multinational companies in palatial
bank and night-clubs. This is where tourists were attracted by
beaches, bazaars and glittering neon lights. But even then, Beirut
was surrounded by a belt of refugee camps and growing slums,
where Palestinian refugees, the Lebanese poor and Syrian 'guest
workers' were crowded together in the shade of the skyscrapers.

Their simmering discontent finally exploded in 1975 with nine-
teen months of street fighting, since when Beirut has been left
like a sick cat too dispirited even to lick its wounds any longer.

On the way down to West Beirut we pass Syrian road blocks
and then drive along the straight road along the seafront towards
the city, and past the airport which is closed due to the fighting.
We enter Ouzai, a slum area inhabited by Palestinian and Lebanese
refugees, the people who have had to flee from the Israeli attacks
on South Lebanon. We pass dilapidated beachclubs, once the
haunts of rich Lebanese and sun-worshipping Western tourists.
Today they are occupied by refugees from Karantina, a slum
wiped out by the right-wing forces during the Civil War. Bombed-
out skeletons of houses, punctured by bullet-holes, serve as
reminders of earlier fighting in this part of the city. But further
in, there are newly-built square blocks of houses that haven't
been affected.

We approach the Cola roundabout, the gateway to the Fakhani
area where the PLO has most of its offices. We slowly wind our
way through an almost static inferno of hooting, dented, ram-
shackle cars. People are milling about, carrying boxes and
suitcases, meandering through the almost non-existent spaces
between the cars. The exhaust fumes are overwhelming and the
noise drowns even the heavy bombardment of East Beirut where
fighting continues.

We slowly drive up the streets towards the Arab University,
past cafes, clothes shops, juice stands and bookshops. The smell
of freshly grilled mutton tickles one's nose while the singing of
Fairouz, the most popular singer in Lebanon, streams from loud-

speakers. At the gate of most houses uniformed Palestinian
soldiers stand with machine guns slung across their shoulders.

This part of West Beirut is called the government area of Palestine in exile, the nerve centre of the PLO. This is where you find
the official Palestinian representatives in different PLO offices —
the information department, the foreign office, the planning
centre, the trade unions, military headquarters, the cultural
department and the Women's Association. Several Palestinian
newspapers are produced in this area, too. The various Palestinian
commando groups in the PLO also have their offices here —
Fatah, the main one, the two Marxist groups, the PFLP (the
People's Front for the Liberation of Palestine) and the DFLP (the
Democratic Front for the Liberation of Palestine), and also
SAIKA (supported by Syria) and the ALF (the Arab Liberation
Front, supported by Iraq). There are also a couple of smaller
groups.

The offices of the PLO and the commando groups are housed
in ordinary blocks of flats. On stairs and in cafes, tenants and
students mingle with Palestinian officials. Agents from all over
the world hide in the crowds. In the summer of 1978, an eight-
storey block here was blown up with 500 pounds of dynamite.
There were several Palestinian offices in the building and 150
people were crushed to death when it collapsed. Nobody knows
exactly who was responsible for the attempt, but it bore the
marks of an Israeli action, according to the Palestinians.

It's an intense, unsettled area. Whilst waiting to meet Palestinian representatives, we came across several foreign journalists
visiting the area for comments, interviews or permission to visit
a refugee camp.

One day, we were sitting in the restaurant of the Women's
Union opposite the Arab University, with Um Leila (one of the
leaders of the Women's Association's Lebanon Department and also
responsible for the day nursery activities in the twelve Palestinian
refugee camps in Lebanon), when suddenly she was called to an
adjacent room only to return a few minutes later.

'A Japanese television team has arrived! They are making a
series on Palestinians and one of their programmes will be about
Palestinian women. They want to film women doing military
training and they want to visit a school. All that's reasonably all
right . . . but do you know what *else* they want?' She drinks her

tea and continues eagerly: 'They have asked me to produce a lovely young Palestinian girl with a beautiful singing voice. They want to film her singing revolutionary songs and playing the guitar, accompanied by a symphony orchestra, on a green meadow with the Mediterranean in the background! I said we have girls who can sing but they play the tablas [drums], according to our tradition. The Japanese wouldn't listen! Then I told them about the only woman I know who plays the guitar. She *is* very beautiful, but has been hit by shrapnel in one eye and has a badly injured right arm. Oh no, they want a *whole*, beautiful girl! Why? What can I do?'

A stylized machine gun on a wall, a common sight in Beirut. The butt is formed of the English letters spelling 'Fatah', the barrel by the Arabic lettering. Fatah is the main commando group and accounts for about 75% of the PLO's armed forces. It is a broad national movement whose aim is the liberation of Palestine and the setting up of a democratic state. While Fatah wants to collaborate with the other Arab regimes against Israel in order to liberate Palestine, the People's Front (the PFLP) and the Democratic Front (the DFLP) are Marxist commando groups, with a Socialist Palestine as their goal. Both also want to unite the Arab masses in a fight against the reactionary Arab regimes, as part of the struggle for the liberation of Palestine. The People's Front reject any negotiation with Israel, which, on the other hand, the Democratic Front would accept.

Um Leila fixes her gaze on the wall, a picture of an old Palestinian woman in traditional dress with a forceful, sad look in her wrinkled face. 'They don't understand. It happens so often when foreigners arrive. They want to give *their* picture of events, not ours! They ask such strange questions . . . and how can we explain?'

2. 'To Be A Palestinian Woman'

One woman we've heard a lot about is Maj Sayyegh — a poetess, Deputy Head of the General Union of Palestinian women and official PLO representative who is almost constantly travelling in the Third World, Europe or the U.S. trying to raise support for the Palestine liberation struggle and its women. Many talk admiringly about her knowledge of women's problems, her dedication and acuteness. A bourgeois woman, others say. One of our male Palestinian friends states with a scornful laugh that she is the woman travelling around in an expensive fur coat lecturing to the poor women in the camps.

We first met Maj in the stark premises of the Women's Association. With its grey-painted walls and furniture upholstered in black PVC, its brown desks with papers and coffee cups littering the worn table-tops, it was rather like many other PLO offices we'd seen. At this, our first meeting, we notice her cool elegance and watchful, critical manner. She was very helpful, like so many women activists. She gave us a routine analysis of the Palestinian refugee problems, and described the difficulties encountered by Palestinian women when they want to get involved in politics. But her time was limited and so we agreed to meet again.

On the next occasion, she dropped her cool official mask when we began to discuss her reactions and feelings, for instance, on meeting Israeli women at international conferences. Then she hesitated for a moment before she said:

> I feel I want to . . . how shall I put it . . . reveal to them, their views on my people, their attitude towards me. I want to show what an oppressive society these women represent, this 'nice' Israeli women's delegation. People think that the Israeli woman is progressive because she does military service,

because she walks the streets in uniform and wears short
skirts. But she never joins the fighting! The Israeli woman is
not progressive, she is oppressed by her regime, and she's
oppressed because she *herself* is an oppressor! Israeli women
helped take our country!

Last year I went to a UN meeting. At first I wasn't going
to speak, but when I saw the Israeli delegation, I changed my
mind. I spoke from a humanitarian point of view, described
how women and children experience oppression. I did not
speak in political terms. It was too much for them and they
left the room.

Her face suddenly grew softer, she groped for the proper
expressions, weighing her words carefully before she spoke, as
she attempted to do justice to the forceful, emotional Arabic
language in English translation. After a brief silence she says:

To be a Palestinian woman always gives me a special feeling.
You know, sometimes I feel I'm transparent . . . the whole
world can pass through me. All the world's sorrow, all suffering. It makes me conscious . . . every day, every second, conscious of everything that takes place before my eyes. I'm
supersensitive to the problems and humiliation of other
peoples. I feel for them what I feel for my own people
. . . for all oppressed people in the world. I believe other
Palestinians feel the same as I do, they care much more about
other people's problems. People here are very conscious, and
that means, they believe they have a role to play during
every second of their lives.

Maj, shrinking slightly into herself, looked vulnerable. Clutching
at her shoulders, it was as if she were trying to protect herself
against the evil of the world.

At first, when I lived in Gaza [the Gaza Strip] and all the
refugees arrived on ships from Northern Palestine after the
State of Israel had been founded in 1948, then I lived among
my own people . . . in Palestine. But at Cairo University I
noticed that some Egyptians deliberately insulted us Palestinians. They didn't know any better! For the first time in
my life I felt like a stranger. I did not identify with the
women who were my friends. When they went to the cinema,

I went to meetings. I felt I had to do something! And I felt bitter.

Maj Sayyegh's face is well-known. Other women activists prefer to remain anonymous in order not to end up on the Israeli photo files.

Maj looked out of the window, shut to exclude the noises from the street.

> I always felt bitter . . . a second-rate human being. But I have a task to perform, a duty to describe my feelings to other people! I write poetry, it's really Palestine I write about, though I base it on my own feelings as a human being. I write about things that all people can associate with . . . home, childhood, surroundings . . . that sort of thing. And about my aspirations for the future. My hopes for the liberation of Palestine!

She straightens her back almost imperceptibly and her hesitation goes.

> I want Palestine to be a place where everybody has a job,

where everybody participates and feels that they belong.
Where everybody can live in peace, in complete equality,
no matter whether they are Muslim, Jewish or Christian;
I'm a Christian myself. A Socialist Palestine! My faith in
righting our wrongs is very strong. My poetry is optimistic
but also melancholy. Sometimes . . . when I feel a deep
sadness, when I can feel everything . . . every pebble in the
street; when I hear and sense unknown things far away. . .
that's when I write . . . . It's difficult. I suffer a lot when I
write, I feel hurt, injured all over my body . . . . I bleed. I
can never be happy with all my heart, the joy may appear
for a short moment but it soon fades . . . .

The room is quiet, very quiet. The air is almost static. Outside
the windows Beirut roars away as thousands of noises form a
constantly changing background. 'Your feelings become a
strength,' she continues. 'They are stronger than you are yourself. They are not inside me, they come from outside, penetrating
me, all the worries of the world . . . the people . . . I don't think
mankind will ever stop suffering!'

This Maj Sayyegh sitting in front of us on the sofa does not
match the initial picture we had of her. Nor does she fit the face-
less picture we have in the West of Palestinians as miserable,
tattered, apathetic refugees or militant fanatics in guerrilla uniforms, spreading terror and destruction with machine guns, bombs
and revolutionary slogans.

When we part company outside the office of the Women's
Association, we decide to meet again, though in fact we never do.
It happens all the time here, it's impossible to make appointments
a long time ahead with anyone working for the 'Revolution', as
the Palestinians call the liberation struggle. Meetings, trips, even
war, intervene and upset all attempts at organized planning.

As we try to hail a taxi, a blue car escorted by two military
jeeps drives up in front of the PLO Foreign Office. A man with
greying hair gets out of the car and disappears into the building,
followed by an armed guard. 'George Habbash, the leader of the
PFLP,' Maj says. 'By the way, did you know that people call this
area the little republic?' She sighs. 'We've had far too many
small republics.'

She is referring to Jordan where the PLO had its headquarters
until 1971 when all overt Palestinian activity was finally crushed
during Black September when thousands upon thousands of

'The crying boy' can be seen in many Palestine homes. He is seen as a symbol of the Palestinian people's suffering.

Palestinians were killed (see the Chronology). At the moment
Lebanon is the only country in the Middle East where Palestinians
still have the right to assert their policy openly.

The cross-section of Palestinians in Lebanon represents the
whole history of their exile. Palestinian activists have found asy-
lum here and we come across women who have even been in
prison in Israel for their resistance. More than a third of the
Palestinians in Lebanon live in refugee camps; they are former
Palestinian smallholders or peasants. The Palestinian middle and
upper classes live in the cities and often have poor contact with
the liberation struggle. They usually have a guilty conscience
about their own lack of involvement. Still, it is these classes that
produce many politically active women, women who have been
educated and have chosen to use their knowledge to serve the
Revolution.

It's frequently said that the middle classes have made
approaches to the peasants since the PLO was formed in 1964
and since armed action increased in the late 1960s. There are rich
Palestinians who support the liberation struggle financially
although they don't take active part in it. The struggle is national,
the aim of the PLO is a free democratic Palestine, which is, of
course, also in the interests of rich Palestinians. A free Palestine
means the possibility of doing business in their home country.

But it's the population of the Palestinian refugee camps that
forms the backbone of the Revolution. It's the camp populations
which are the victims of Israeli aggression. It's the men and women
in the camps who give their lives and die for the freedom they
uphold. It's the camp women who send their sons to the mountains to join the guerrillas. And the PLO administrators always long
to go to the camps and the guerrillas. For that's where the struggle
is alive and where they get the strength to continue.

We visited almost all the refugee camps — Bourj al Barajneh,
Shatila and Sabra in Beirut, Nahr al Bared and Baddawi outside Tripoli
in North Lebanon, Damour south of Beirut, Ain al Helweh and Miye
outside Saida and Bourj al Shemaleh and al Bass in the Sour area of
South Lebanon. But it was Rashidiyeh, south of Sour, where we
spent six weeks with the camp women and their families.

3. 'After The Revolution We Were Reborn'

We travelled down towards Southern Lebanon in a group taxi together with Mouna, a young Palestinian woman with bushy black hair and laughing eyes which could very quickly turn serious. She was twenty-three and responsible for the local department of the Palestine Women's Union in the area around the Lebanese port of Sour, 20 kilometres north of the Israeli border. In the Sour area there are 40,000 Palestinian refugees in three different camps. Rashidiyeh is the one where Mouna lives.

We followed the main road along the Mediterranean, where the traffic was heavy and noisy and where our driver overtook other cars as if death did not concern him. There were almost as many wrecked cars along the road as there were bombed-out, burnt-out houses. The Civil War has left deep, unhealed wounds on buildings as well as people.

In the blackened ruins of a petrol station, a man was selling cigarettes and whisky. He had made a painstaking pyramid arrangement of cigarette cartons and had polished the whisky bottles until they shone.

A good half hour's drive south of Beirut, we passed through Damour, a ruined town clinging to the mountainside. Ghostly, blown-up houses with gaping windows, some temporarily covered with plastic sheets that flapped in the wind, came into view. There is laundry on the balconies, and the walls are covered with Arabic graffiti: *'Down With Imperialism'*, *'Palestine, Your People Is Coming'*, *'Revolution To Victory'*. We saw everywhere posters, faces of men or groups of men with machine guns held high — martyr posters of Palestinian liberation heroes killed in action.

'There are Palestinians living in these ruins,' Mouna said. 'We call Damour the widows' town, because 70% of the adult population are widows. Their husbands died in the battle of Tal al Zaatar, a refugee camp in East Beirut. The right wing wiped out Tal al Zaatar in 1976. The surviving Palestinians were taken here to Damour. The town had been evacuated since the Palestinians and the Lebanese left wing had taken it from the right earlier on in the civil war.'

Women in the widows' town of Damour. There is a great surplus of women in the camps, because so many Palestinian men have been killed in the liberation war.

Mouna, looking out of the open car window, watched the people moving in the streets among the ruins. 'I suffer when I go through Damour. Damour is not even a camp, it's much worse!' Her hoarse voice breaks. 'Our camps are well organized but we haven't had time to do anything yet about Damour. In Tal al Zaatar the Women's Union had done a lot of work many women there were active. We had committees, day nurseries, sewing classes, literacy classes, in the same way as we have in all camps. It had taken a long time to build up, *years* of hard

17

work. It was *all* destroyed, levelled to the ground. That's our
situation. The projects we start are constantly threatened by era-
dication, we can never trust that something we've built up will
be allowed to stand.'

Her shrug was not one of defeat, but one we were often to see.
'You can see the problems we have to contend with. Here, in
Damour, we shall have to start again from scratch. We are constantly uprooted. Old women in Damour have already had to flee
five or six times and no one knows whether they'll have to flee
once more . . . .'

'Look,' she said, pointing at some totally collapsed houses on
the right towards the sea.

> The Israeli bombs! Not only did they take our country, they
> are still hounding us. For thirty-one years . . . just because
> we want to return to our homes! We are stateless! Compared
> to that, all the other problems seem to shrink. The women,
> women's struggle, has a long way to go when the whole
> people is oppressed. Not even the men are free! As long as
> there is no base for a structure, nothing will work out as we
> want it. We don't even have a country or an economy of our
> own . . . so how can we possibly solve our social and econo-
> mic problems? In the West you've had plenty of time to
> solve your problems and you also live in peace. That's
> different!
>
> We have a lot in common with women of the Third World.
> We share the fight against imperialism and colonialism. Here
> in the Middle East imperialism is expressed through Zionism,
> which believes that all the Jews of the world should have a
> state of their own, Israel, in *our* home country of Palestine!
> The Zionists also think of Southern Lebanon as belonging
> to them! We Palestinian women suffer from the same poverty
> and social and religious oppression as the women of the Third
> World. But they at least live in *their own* countries. Whereas
> all the Palestinians are scattered in many, many different
> countries . . . .

Just beyond Saida we pass the last Syrian road block on the way
south. As always, at Syrian road blocks, all conversation in the
car stops and the radio is turned off. The traffic slows down,
one car after another is lazily waved past, but our car is stopped

and the Syrian soldier asks to see everybody's identity cards. He leafs through our passports from the back, nods with authority when he reaches the passport pictures and waves us on. The man in the front seat swears. Nobody likes the Syrians.

'Now we are in the liberated part of Lebanon,' said Mouna with a broad smile. 'Here the Lebanese left wing and the Palestinians rule. But further south Haddad has control. Haddad is a Lebanese Fascist working with the Zionists against us. He shells at the camps.'

Since the Palestinians took control of the camps, the camp militia can be seen everywhere.

On this occasion, neither Mouna nor I can know that in April 1979 Major Saad Haddad, the leader of the right-wing forces in Southern Lebanon will, on his own initiative, proclaim an 'independent' state — 'The Free Lebanon' — on the strip of land, ten kilometres wide, which he controls on this side of the Israeli border. Neither do we know that the Israelis together with the right-wing forces are for most of 1979 to bomb and shell the Palestinian refugee camps and Lebanese villages in Southern Lebanon.

19

'By the way,' she continued, 'do you know that we call the camps liberated areas? The PLO took control of all camps in 1968 when we had the Revolution. We say that before the Revolution we were living dead and after the Revolution we were reborn.'

Mouna, with many gestures, talked on. She told us that the PLO was founded in 1964, that Palestinians carried out the first armed action inside Israel during the following year, 1965. Then, during the war of June 1967 the Arab armies were conquered by Israel. But the Palestinians still continued with their armed action against Israel, although the Arab regimes had started 'pointless' negotiations with Israel and the USA. 'We were the only ones who did anything!' Mouna exclaimed. 'That's why we became so popular with many Arabs. Not only Palestinians joined the PLO but also Syrians, Lebanese, Egyptians, Iraqis, yes, people from all Arab countries!'

She described how the PLO became stronger and stronger, how more and more actions were carried out and how the camp populations were given arms when the PLO took over the camps.

> We Palestinians retrieved some of our self-respect. We could defend ourselves! Today there is in fact a machine gun in each house in the camps. What would have happened if we hadn't armed ourselves? If we hadn't started the guerrilla actions? The world would have forgotten us! And no one would have reminded the world if *we* hadn't. Certainly not the Zionists! The Zionists would have been pleased to see us rotting away in our camps without resisting.
>
> And what did the UN do, letting the Zionists take our country? After the flight from Palestine in 1948, no one wanted to have anything to do with us, not even the Arab countries! Here in Lebanon the Lebanese put us in camps and the UN formed UNRWA [the United Nations Relief and Welfare Agency] to administer the camps. That was because the Lebanese refused to pay, although they were happy to guard us.

Mouna told us that the Lebanese fenced in many camps with barbed wire, and sent officials and agents from the Lebanese Security Service into the camps. They refused the Palestinians the right to move out, they preferred to have them all under control in a few places, to stop the Palestinians competing with the Lebanese on the labour market. UNRWA provided the Palestinians with food rations up to a level of bare subsistence. Mouna also said that her grandfather used to sneak out of the camp to find jobs on the black labour market. Many others did the same. 'UNRWA built schools where we Palestinians had no right to make decisions. Before the Revolution in 1968, not a word about Palestine was mentioned in the schools. *That* was the contribution of the UN!'

Outside the car window, orange groves and banana plantations, partly concealed by high cypresses, swept past. 'It looks like Northern Palestine,' Mouna said slowly. 'Like Galilee where I come from. I've never been there, but my grandmother and grandfather can tell you about it! For thousands of years we have been a farming people, for thousands of years we have worked and tilled the soil of Palestine. It is the Zionists who have made the world believe that Palestine was a desert until they arrived! Do you know how long it takes before an olive tree bears fruit? Fifty years! Today the Israelis are selling *our* olives! And they export *our* Jaffa oranges!'

The man on the front seat intervenes: 'Yes, but you'll find the same kind of oranges here in Lebanon. The Jaffa oranges are not an Israeli invention, they are Arabic.' He is Lebanese, but like many others in Southern Lebanon he supports the Palestinian cause. He sees the Israelis as a threat and the Lebanese right wing as traitors.

Mouna continued:

> The oranges and the olives and the land we owned in Palestine were our capital. The Zionists took it away from us! We escaped without any money. The middle class people in the towns had money, not to mention the upper classes . . . . We're no different from other peoples, they could buy themselves houses, rent flats and buy jobs. But we, the smallholders, had nothing, we were forced to the camps!

Mouna stopped talking, reflected for a moment and lighted a cigarette.

> But today many of us want to stay in the camps. Leaving would be the same as giving up Palestine! We will not be incorporated with Lebanon! *Never*! We are Palestinians! We want to go home! To Palestine! I'm fighting for that,

every moment I spend working among the women in the camps. I'm telling you because I want you to understand!

We arrived at Sour, the Biblical town of Tyre, once visited by Christ. The 70 kilometres from Beirut have taken us two hours on a road that is badly maintained and very busy. We change to another group taxi which will take us the last three kilometres south to Rashidiyeh.

Dusk is falling as we leave Sour. We pass one of the headquarters of UNIFIL (the United Nations Interim Forces in Lebanon). Through the gates we see Senegalese UN soldiers in blue berets wandering about amongst the white UN jeeps and light armoured vehicles. The UN are in Southern Lebanon to 'hold the peace'. But the Israeli forces keep flying over their areas and Haddad fires at the UN bases.

'This road continues down towards Palestine, but I musn't go any further,' Mouna said as we turned off into a small road on the right. 'Further south the right wing would shoot me.' We have arrived at Rashidiyeh.

4. The Refugee Camp of Rashidiyeh

We are stopped at a little sentry-box at the entrance of Rashidiyeh. A few guards in green uniforms, armed with machine guns, watch us suspiciously. 'They are friends,' Mouna says. We show them our permits from the PLO office in Beirut with the PLO stamp at the top. A long conversation follows in Arabic between Mouna and the guards.

'*Ahlan wa sahlan!*' — Welcome, they eventually say, and their faces break into broad smiles. A bearded guard runs into the orange grove to get us some newly picked oranges. They ask us to stay and have tea with them. We say we can't but will come back later.

They are always very suspicious of strangers, Westerners. It's a matter of security, Mouna says later. 'Always carry your papers when you walk round the camp. The camp militia are all over the place and you will be stopped every now and then.'

It grows dark very quickly and the few little shops along the road are lit by naked bulbs. Outside are groups of people. It looks like any village, a cluster of small houses with lanes meandering down a hillside. The taxi driver routinely avoids the large round holes in the asphalt. 'Shell holes,' Mouna explains, 'they are everywhere. You'll see enough evidence of Israeli bombings. But it's been quiet now for a long time . . . still . . . how much longer?'

We drive through what is now called the old camp, with its long history. Rashidiyeh means 'the wise man' and it was an ordinary Lebanese village at the turn of the century. After the First World War, however, when England and France re-drew the map of the Middle East, Turkey was granted a small area in Northern Syria around the port of Iskanderoun. Many Syrians left and escaped south towards Lebanon, finally ending up at Rashidiyeh. Thirty years later the Palestine refugees came to

Rashidiyeh, reinforcing the village's status as a refugee camp.

Rashidiyeh — the new camp. In the background the port of Sour (Tyre).

We pass an open field and see the school on a hill to the right as we drive up to the new camp, where long straight lanes cross each other in a regular formation of square blocks. The new camp was built in the 1960s by the Palestinians, aided by the UN.

When we get out of the taxi, we can hear the surf pounding the Mediterranean shore a few streets away. Mouna greets a tall man with grey hair. 'This is Abu Ahmed, the Chairman of the People's Committee in Rashidiyeh.' The People's Committee is a cross between a village council and a district council, consisting of ten elected representatives of the different guerrilla groups and a highly esteemed independent village elder who has a function similar to that of the *mukhtar* (mayor) in the Palestinian villages. The committee is responsible for the management of the camp. It meets regularly and discusses different issues, such as the school, the shelters, refuse disposal or possible internal conflicts, whenever it is possible to intervene. The committee can also function as a sort of local court for petty crime committed in the camp.

We turn off into one of the straight lanes. It has grown dark now and there is no street lighting. The little windows of the houses do not give enough light for us to see the way. 'Yes,' Mouna says, as we stumble forward, 'it is dark. We don't want to make it any easier for Israeli planes or gunboats to find the camp at night — in case they decide to do a raid under cover of darkness.'

She opens a squeaky metal gate and we enter an open courtyard and walk through the door of a small room. There we find Mouna's family — children, parents and grandparents, sitting on mattresses with flowery patterns, eating from bowls on a green oilcloth, spread out on the floor. The children shout in delight, they rush up and throw themselves around Mouna's neck. She bends down towards an old woman whose shining, wrinkled cheeks are marked with blue tattoos. Mouna kisses the woman twice on each cheek and hugs her warmly. The woman peers at us inquiringly. 'My grandmother! She is very old, no one knows quite how old. She is a living history book.'

A pregnant woman stands up and waits smiling, her arms extended. She holds Mouna tight. 'This is my mother, Um Immad!' says Mouna laughing. 'I have only been away overnight, but my family always welcome me as if I had been gone for years. Such are our Arabic customs, we always show how much we mean to each other!'

An old man with a white headshawl mutters something, bending his head reverently. Mouna nods. He is her grandfather, but they do not touch each other. Young women do not embrace old men. She doesn't embrace her brother either, he just nods kindly over his books and notepads. 'My eldest brother — he is eighteen and training to be an engineer in Sour. His name is Immad. Mother is called Um Immad, it means mother of Immad, for according to our tradition, the mother and father take the name of their eldest son. I am four years older, but a *girl*. That's how it is. Although we're in the middle of a liberation struggle, our traditions are very hard to change.'

Um Immad interrupts, asking us to sit down and eat. Everybody watches us carefully but amicably. Mouna keeps talking in English, translating her words into Arabic for the rest of the family. 'Palestine, you see, was a very patriarchal society, and my people are still in the firm grip of those traditions,' Mouna eagerly explains. 'Unfortunately, the women have to sacrifice themselves to make it easier for the men. Look at our Palestinian leaders, they are all men! They think that women's liberation is something that will have to wait, it mustn't get in the way of the national liberation struggle. They seem to believe that the one excludes the other, but I think they could both go hand in hand. But it's *not* easy! You'll soon see for yourselves, if you spend some time here . . . .'

We were to spend many evenings with this family. Throughout our stay in Rashidiyeh, Mouna was our friend and interpreter, a person who constantly clarified and explained the society in which she lived, in order to help us understand it better.

5. The Teardrop Becomes a Dagger

A noticeable stillness hovered over the dawn on the following day. The Mediterranean was rolling towards the shore as the sky grew brighter in the east. Then the loudspeaker of the minaret crackled, and a few seconds later the ancient message of Islam, monotonous and persistent, filled the air over the thousands of flat roofs in Rashidiyeh.

'*Allah akbaar . . . Allah akbaar . . .*' — God is great . . . God is immense . . . The religious chant echoed out over the light green fields and orange groves surrounding the camp, fading over the cypress avenues between the orchards, continuing down towards the mountains in the south, and disappearing in the rolling waves.

The chanting of Allah's greatness mingled with the crowing of the cocks to wake the 15,000 Palestinian refugees living here. Such is the rhythm of 'quiet' and 'peaceful' days — even if peace in itself is still only a vision to the Palestinians, a shimmering goal lying somewhere far in the future.

On the roof of her house, Mouna is taking the morning air. Around the edge of the roof terrace, you can see the points of reinforcing girders. Three years ago the house was hit by an Israeli grenade and had to be rebuilt. It's still not quite finished, like so many other things in the camp. Mouna is deep in thought with her arms folded on her chest. Hanging from a thin gold chain around her neck is a golden miniature map of Palestine, which looks like a teardrop, apparently alighting briefly against her skin before falling to the ground. She moves, the drop gleams in the morning sun, suddenly aspected as a pointed dagger. Many young men and women wear such an amulet, often with a miniature Koran dangling from the same chain. Mouna has only the map of Palestine. She has done with religion and no longer believes that Allah has the power to help her people, as she did when she was younger and prayed to Allah the required five times each day.

Minutes pass and women's voices are heard calling to each other. Tousled, newly awakened children open the gate on to the narrow street. Older men in traditional Arab dress — a *gallabiya* (a full-length garment) and a *koffiya* (head shawl) — start pottering through the alleys, watching the group taxis drive slowly past the field to transport commuters to work in Sour. The cars turn at the water-channel where some girls have already gathered to wash last night's dishes before having breakfast and going to school. The camp is no longer still.

This morning, as on other mornings, Mouna awoke before the rest of her family. Yet, the night before she had been the last one to fall asleep. In a refugee camp, you're surrounded every second by others; you constantly hear the neighbouring family talk or quarrel through the partition or over the wall to the courtyard. The concrete houses stand close together, and the large families with many children live in crowded and cramped conditions. Mouna finds peace and solitude only when her seven younger brothers and sisters, mother and grandparents are asleep. That is when she reads political papers, books and pamphlets published by the PLO on the Palestinian struggle. But there are only two books on Palestinian women. She has to find her examples of fighting women in the USSR and the Third World, and draw her inspiration from women in Algeria, Vietnam, China and Cuba.

And she needs strength and self-confidence for her work amongst the women. Strength to resist patriarchal tradition, strength not to break down and become paralysed when the camps are bombed, strength to give support to others and strength to go on fighting for her people's liberation, all this to which she has devoted her life.

'*Sabah al Kher Mouna!*' — Good morning, her grandmother shouts from the courtyard below.

'*Sabah al noor! Kif halik?*' Mouna replies. The light of the morning! How are you?

'*Al hamdulilla! Kif halik inte?*' Praise to God! How are you? the old lady continues.

'*Kwayes, tamman,*' says Mouna. Very well!

They exchange the obligatory ritual of the morning and the old woman goes on watering the sage bushes and other plants growing in discarded rusty tins. Everywhere in the camp courtyards, there are rows of potted plants. Mouna's younger brothers and sisters put on their beige school coats and two of the girls help Um

Immad pile the mattresses against the wall in one of the two small rooms allocated to the family. At night five children sleep close together on mattresses on the floor, just as all the families in the camp do.

Immad, the eldest brother, searches for the news on the radio in order to hear the latest developments. Like all Palestinians, he follows the news carefully. With the radio going, the family gathers for breakfast, sitting on the floor in the Arab way. Mouna pours them tea, weak and of poor quality, but its taste improves with some sage and two large spoonfuls of sugar in each little tea glass. Green olives, olive oil with thyme and thin white bread are eaten for breakfast. Each person places the bread on their lap, tears off a piece and folds it around the thyme mixture. No cutlery, no plates are used, but communal bowls are shared by everyone.

Um Immad makes sure that everyone eats. She is thirty-eight, and has had fifteen 'tummies' as Arabs say when a women has had fifteen children. Nine of them are still alive, six died of diseases

at a tender age. Now she is six months pregnant, with her
sixteenth child. She was thirteen when she had her first baby,
Mouna's elder sister. Her face is covered by fine little wrinkles
and often has an expression of pain and suffering.

'Mouna, what was Beirut like this time?' she asks, frowning
as she often does. Beirut is a sensitive matter. Mouna travels the
70 kilometres there once a week to meet representatives of the
different Women's Committees in the camps and then spends the
night there. In a Muslim community it is against all rules that a
single woman should spend the night in a strange city, without
parents, without being watched over by a brother or a close
relation. But a refugee's life, with its constant decampments and
fighting, affects tradition. Old customs are challenged but die
slowly, and Mouna's adult life has been a struggle to change the
customs.

Six years ago, when Mouna first started her active work, she'd
have to sneak off to the meetings of the Women's Committee in
the camp. She would lie to her parents, saying that she was doing
her homework together with her friend Shahirah when, in fact,
both were going to the meetings and had to hide the papers in
their school-books. After some time Mouna began to talk to Um
Immad, explaining carefully and patiently to her mother, who is
illiterate, that it's important for women, too, to take part in the
struggle. 'In other countries, the women take part, the Israeli
women are educated and knowledgeable. Why should they be
stronger? We are not any more stupid than they, we've got brains
too! We have to do the same thing! Educate our women! We
can't grow strong while half of us — the women — only stay at
home.'

Mouna's mother listened reluctantly but with mounting
interest. She tried to understand and accept that times have
changed since she herself grew up in a Palestinian farming community which did not encourage women. Today Um Immad is very
supportive and she puts her foot down if neighbours or relations
make critical remarks about her daughter who has chosen the
liberation struggle instead of marriage and raising a family.

Her father, Abu Immad, however, initially refused to listen.
He was very critical and resentful of Mouna's involvement, even
though he works for Fatah and delivers food to the guerrilla bases,
coming home only once a fortnight. 'When I told him *one* word
about my activities, he would respond with a thousand! Politics
are for men and women should encourage the men to be even

Liberation! Victory! The message is an armed struggle for peace in this women's poster. In Palestinian symbolism the women usually fight for peace and the men for justice.

more active. He didn't altogether mind if other women got involved — but not his own daughter! Like all men he feared that I might be taken for a slut, one of those who join the Revolution to meet men! Oh yes, that's what people think! But now he's changed his mind. Mother talked to him,' she says triumphantly, with a giggle.

Today Abu Immad's respect for Mouna's work is growing. She is also the only woman member of the local Fatah council in Sour and helps make decisions on the management of the camps and the organization of military activities. 'When I came back from Moscow,' Mouna says, 'I felt reborn. During a whole year I had been treated with unquestioned respect.'

6. Villages Are Turned into 'Areas'

The children can be seen everywhere in the alleys of the camp, busy throwing stones through the bullet-holes in the wall of a bombed-out house, or gathered round the rusty wreck of a car which they pretend is an Israeli bomber. Though they have grown up with the Israeli bombers and know well enough that the Palestinians have none, when they play, Israelis and Palestinians are equally strong. We hear the children's shrill voices as they slide down the entrance to a shelter or when the boys play football in the open field down by the sea.

During our first days in the camp, we seem to be followed everywhere by the children. '*Yalla! Yalla!*' — Come! Come! '*Ajnabiya!*' — Stranger! Other children come streaming from the alleys, yelling. 'Hello! Hello! How are you? What is your name? What are you? . . . What are you doing? What is this? Hello!' The children are all shouting at once in English, with a strong accent. The older children remain in the background and the adults stand by their gates, although they all keep a watchful eye on us. '*Ahlein! Ahlein!*' — Welcome! '*Faddal!*' — Come in! they say with a sweeping gesture towards the courtyard. We are offered a glass of tea, or Arabic coffee if we prefer it. This is repeated at every gate. After a while we have to turn down these friendly invitations.

But the children cling to us like leeches. We walk down to the sea to find some peace. The alley ends at a barrier, manned by the camp militia. One of the guards nods towards us, we have met before and he knows who we are. '*Yalla!*' — Run off! Go away! he shouts at the children. But the boys follow us out onto the shore and turn somersaults in the sand which whirls in the wind. They walk on their hands or provoke loud belches to the delight of the others. It's impossible to be left alone.

We Shall Return!

'*Saura! Saura! Saurina!*' — Take a picture! A picture! they
shout when they see our cameras. They all stand to attention in
front of the camera, stiff and tense. Some make the sign of victory
and others follow. With serious faces they make the sign for the
liberation of Palestine.

Later on, we laugh over the episode and tell Mouna about the
children who followed us so closely. She listens attentively. 'We're
not used to seeing Westerners. Strangers. Most of us can't afford
ever to leave the camp. In your country you can afford to go on
holidays. We are referred to our camps.' Her eyes are bitter.
'It was the isolation of the camp that followed you around. Not
the children!'

The isolation in the camps has another aspect: Rashidiyeh and
other camps have become a simulacrum of the old Palestinian
countryside, little Palestines in exile where the populations from
the scattered villages have congregated once more and formed
their own areas within the camp. Here the 'village' lives on,
relations live next door to each other, and people prefer to inter-
marry within the 'village' following the old prescriptions for
cousins to marry.

This also means that old conflicts and discord between the
'villages' have survived, even though no one can remember why
or how they started. Perhaps it was access to a watercourse long
ago. Sometimes the old quarrel has almost turned into a ritual:
an expression of the Palestinians' refusal to accept that their
traditional farming communities have been pulled up by the roots
and have crumbled away. The plots of land, no larger than allot-
ments, leased by a few around Rashidiyeh are no proper replace-
ment for the land they lost in their native country. Neither are the
little tins with potted sage plants.

They all lost their former life, but the men have been forced to
look for work in Lebanon in a labour market rife with discri-
mination against Palestinians. Only 7% of the women work outside
the home. The others stay in their courtyards or nearby in the
same area. Only rarely do they venture beyond it and hardly ever
do they go outside the camp. That is why the memories and the
culture of the home country are mainly preserved by the women.

There is not one single telephone in Rashidiyeh. Mail is deli-
vered sporadically and is then placed on the bonnet of a car outside the UN premises where the camp children are fed. News from
outside comes from the men who have been out at work during
the day, or from the children who go to training courses outside

the camp. When friends or relatives from outside come visiting, this is an important event, which attracts many listeners. All this has the effect that the women are not directly confronted with the society outside the camp during more peaceful periods.

It has now been calm for months and the camp is functioning well. Everybody knows that this lull is only temporary. It may last for another month, perhaps two months, or even more. But there could also be a raid tomorrow. Perhaps even tonight! The constant uncertainty and the anxiety brought on by it are always there beneath the surface. Every day! Year after year!

What seems more strange to us is the fact that life continues. It has to continue, it's a matter of survival. But it is a life that is literally a struggle between life and death; with death always present and natural, and one where you simply replace the dead by giving birth to new life. A life where nothing is indifferent, where every action is born in pain. A life where every emotion finds its own release, without inhibition, and one where other people are always at hand with support, good advice and affection. A life where the roles are predetermined by religious dogma and one where each person knows their place and function.

But at the same time it is a life where the roles are changing. A life which has become revolutionary, and one where there is nothing to lose.

7. The Street As Woman's Kingdom

When the children have gone to school, Um Immad is left with the youngest children and their grandmother. Mouna is out working and Grandfather has gone out to chat with the other old men. During the day Um Immad and the other women reign supreme in the camp. She does her housework which takes a long time because of the lack of modern household appliances — these exist only in American films on television, though many households do, in fact, have both a television set and cassette player.

The women have to carry their children about, yet they still have to bend down to sweep the floor or wash clothes in the muddy ditch full of infected water. They also have to make bread several times a week, working with up to twenty pounds of flour at a time. But although they are always busy there is a continuous murmur of chatter with the neighbouring women for all doors and gates are open. They visit each other constantly or sit working together in groups.

On our first morning, Um Immad was separating green olives from black ones. Later, she will salt and preserve this food, so indispensable to a Palestinian household. The vines over the courtyard provide shade during the hot summer days, but now, in the autumn, leaves with brown edges fall rustling gently to the concrete floor.

There is a loud knock at the door and Um Immad raises her head, tucking in a lock of her greying black hair under the headscarf. A man in a worn jacket steps across the threshold. His head is wrapped in several layers of a red and white *koffiya*, in the way that workers wear their headshawl. This is Abu Mohammed who is to dig a gully between Um Immad's house and the house next door. They have been expecting him for weeks, but no one is irritated. Few things here work according to schedule.

Arab food is plentiful and takes a long time to cook, but the people in the camp have simple eating habits. The basic foods are rice and lentils, with some mutton or chicken. Muslims do not eat pork which is considered to be unclean.

This gully will help them, for Um Immad and her daughters will not, any longer, have to throw dirty water directly into the alley or have to go to the large drainage ditch some houses away. This family is one of the last in the camp to have the problem of drainage sorted out.

Um Immad calls her sister-in-law next door. She comes out at once, carrying her youngest daughter and together they go into the alley to discuss the details of the digging of the gully. Grandmother follows with great interest. Grandfather is already waiting outside the house. Um Abdullah appears, a large, erect woman, as so many of them are. Her stride is heavy and determined. From a distance she has sensed that something is happening at Um Immad's house. As for Um Ali in the opposite house, she can stay calmly where she is by her basin of vegetables. She watches the events with her youngest son sitting close to his mother, playing quietly with little stones, his bottom bare.

Many curious people gather round the man who is to dig the gully. He turns the first sods. Two men from the camp militia in green uniform, platform shoes, machine guns slung over their shoulders, give their points of view and offer everyone cigarettes, as is the custom if you smoke yourself. Everyone interferes, everyone wants to help, in a refugee camp it's become quite natural for everyone to contribute something.

The shovelled sand piles up and Um Immad seems to grow at the same rate. Her bearing has suddenly changed, her tired face has become animated: the woman who is usually so gentle now has a commanding look. It is, after all, *her* gully that is being dug! For this brief moment, she is one of the central characters and the digging will continue for four days before the gully is completed!

Events like this are spectacles, occasions on which to drink tea and exchange views. On this occasion they all talk about President Sadat and his deception of the Palestinians in starting negotiations with Israel. Nobody believes that this will bring any benefits. 'Sadat is an arse! A bloody arsehole! A traitor,' Um Abdullah says, slapping the bottom of Abu Mohammed who is leaning forward, digging. Everybody laughs heartily and agrees. Joking is a way of socializing. The women make jokes on all subjects and can often be quite crude.

On the walls in the camp there are many anti-Sadat slogans next to slogans against Zionism, against imperialism, against the politics of the reactionary Arab states. These are constant topics of conversation, not only amongst the men but equally amongst the women. Discussions are often heated.

A rattling lorry parks beside a bombed-out house at the nearest junction. The chicken lorry has arrived! Hens' eyes stare out between the platform rails. The group around the gully have something new to watch and people flock quickly around the truck. Um Ali in the house opposite swears angrily when she upsets her basin of cut vegetables. A stream of accusations is directed against her baby son who is not to blame at all. He puts a sandy piece of tomato in his mouth and looks anxiously around. Um Ali shuffles into the house on her clapping plastic sandals, collecting money to buy chickens.

The chicken dealer matter-of-factly cuts one chicken throat after another weighing the live body on his scales. The women pay with old, almost furry bank-notes, which have been circulating in the camp for a long time. The chicken dealer throws down each flapping body to die in the sand of the alley. The children study the death struggle in fascination, though they have already seen it many times. Most children have grown up with death, some of them have even seen their fathers killed in front of their eyes.

Suddenly two white bands are seen against the clear blue sky. 'Phantoms! Phantoms! *Tayran!*' — Aeroplanes! Israelis! the children shout. Um Ali's eyes widen and she automatically picks up her baby from the ground, holding her arms around him. Mouna's grandmother clasps her hands towards the sky, calling on Allah and cursing the Israelis in the same breath. The little boys raise an invisible machine gun firing at the planes in the air. The chicken dealer goes on with his slaughter. 'Our Palestinian soldiers are fighting the Zionists! We are strong and we'll regain

our country. This is what our soldiers will do to the Zionists'
throats,' the chicken dealer says, cutting yet another hen's throat.
Some of the women urge him on.

Every day the Israeli military aircraft fly over Rashidiyeh, sometimes several times a day. When they are as high up as they were
on that occasion, it is only a reconnaissance flight, they all know
that. But, more than anything else, they all fear the fighter
bombers. For they are small and swift and they can fly low. There
is never time to go to the shelters before the first bombs fall on
people and houses.

One finds the traces of earlier raids everywhere in Rashidiyeh.
Further along the alley are a couple of houses bombed to the
ground. They had been inhabited until the Israeli invasion of
Southern Lebanon in March 1978. Then the Israelis crossed the
border with infantry and armoured vehicles, with aircraft and gun-
boats. They were only a few kilometres south of Rashidiyeh.
The Israelis bombed the camps and completely destroyed several
Lebanese mountain villages. They succeeded in scaring away the
population, and managed to force the evacuation of Southern
Lebanon. The people in Rashidiyeh fled. Altogether 300,000
Palestinians and Lebanese escaped north to the 'safety' of Beirut.
There they had to live in temporary tent camps, bombed houses,
school buildings. Most of them returned within two months, but
some of them never came back.

It wasn't the first Israeli attempt to chase away the population.
Beside the sea in Rashidiyeh are three rows of houses which have
been totally destroyed. In 1974-75 these houses were bombed to
smithereens, mainly by gunboats at sea. The Israelis tried to land
troops but failed. The weeds are growing among the empty spooky
ruins, but the ruins have been left as a defence line against
renewed attacks from the sea. One of the buildings had been
inhabited by some of Um Immad's relations. They never returned.
The man managed to find a job in Beirut and today his family
are living in a dark little flat behind a garage in the house where
he works as a caretaker. However, he still visits Rashidiyeh as
often as he can afford to although his wife and children remain
in Beirut, since they don't have enough money for them all to
travel as is so often the case. The men travel alone.

'In Rashidiyeh I'm among my people,' he says. 'Here I breathe
Palestine!' Many of the Palestinians who have moved out of the

camp express the same view. After all, it's in the camps that you can find the security of your own people, this is where you find the solidarity and togetherness of the vulnerable.

The electricity system. 'Whatever we do is provisional — the Israelis can start bombing at any moment.'

8. Why Mouna's Grand-mother Sold her Jewellery

It's one of many evenings at Um Immad's. Abu Immad is at home. He is sitting in a corner, gently smoking his *nargila*, a water-pipe. Um Immad places a small piece of live coal on the pressed tobacco. Abu Immad sucks at the mouthpiece, the water in the water-pipe gurgles, and the glass is filled with smoke. A sweet smell of tobacco spreads through the room. After a little while he hands the mouthpiece to his father.

From the room next door one can hear the sound of the television. In Southern Lebanon you can only get Israeli television which has news in Arabic every evening and one Arabic feature film a week. Everyone will meet together to watch it. They often show films from Egypt, the Arab country which produces most films. But whilst we were listening the Muppet Show was on in English with Hebrew subtitles. No one showed any interest in the strange puppets.

Mouna took out her machine gun from the cupboard, and sat down on the floor to clean it, carefully oiling each part. A couple of her younger brothers and sisters watch every move she makes. They know how to do it, too, as both of them go to a military training course where they have learnt to dismantle and put together a machine gun in less than one minute.

Granny, waking from a nap, looks at Mouna: 'It's a good thing that women learn to carry weapons,' she says suddenly from where she is sitting on the floor. 'But not all feel as I do, they believe it's up to the men. A lot of things have changed for women since the Revolution. I can see that, because I'm so old.' She looks at her husband and son at the water-pipe. 'When I was young the women used to keep to themselves, and the men too. We girls were sewing and chatting among ourselves. I hadn't even seen my husband before we got married. Today the girls are asked what they think, and today women even lead military operations into Palestine.'

The old lady begins to tell us about her early days in Palestine:

> In the evenings my mother used to tell stories to the
> children. Heroic tales! The heroes were courageous: Sinbad,
> Hadadoun, Al Beydin . . . and Hassan — he helped the poor
> . . . . We lived happily in Palestine, but now we are poor.
> One of my neighbours said that the Germans don't know
> what happened to us Palestinians. Nor do the Americans!
> You must tell them what we want!

How often we've heard the old people expressing themselves in this way! They urge us to explain to other Westerners what has happened to the people of Palestine. When we come across older Palestinians, we barely have time to greet them before they start telling us about their lost home country. They are not resigned, on the contrary, they consider it necessary to explain and justify the war that their children and grandchildren are conducting against Israel. We are made to understand that the liberation of Palestine is not just a question of returning home, it is also a matter of regaining their human dignity and respect in the eyes of other people. 'You live in your country. How can you realize the grief of losing your home country?' Grandmother says slowly and deliberately. 'When I go down to the beach I can see Palestine, the last headland to the south, where Nakoura is.'

But this headland is like a wall: behind it lie only memories, for no Palestinian in Rashidiyeh can legally cross the border of their old home country. Along the entire boundary between Lebanon and Israel there runs an electrified fence of barbed wire, which is supplemented in places by a mine field and, on the Israeli side, by a wide band of well-raked gravel to reveal footprints.

'*We* can't go back,' Mouna says quietly, 'but a Jew from New York can automatically become a citizen . . . .'

'*W'Allah*'. By Allah! 'If they offered me the whole of Southern Lebanon, I wouldn't have it,' Granny says fervently. 'I want to go home! We are farmers! We grew figs, olives, apricots, tomatoes and tobacco in different fields around the village. We lived in a stone cottage with vaulted ceilings and five rooms. I remember all our goats, the sheep and the hens . . . .'

'And the mare,' Grandfather interrupts, sucking his water-pipe. 'That was nice, a mare in those days was like having a

Cadillac now.'

They dream about seeing their farm in Palestine again. Often
the old folk don't realize that the farm they left in 1948 has long
since been levelled to the ground. The Israelis have carefully and
systematically erased over 400 Palestinian villages from the map.
But the memory of their home village has been imprinted in
children and grandchildren. When we ask Palestinian children
where they were born, they will answer with the name of a village
in Palestine where their parents came from. Everyone knows and
no one forgets.

The children switch off the television and join us. They are
sitting still and listening attentively. There is a great respect for the
old. 'I remember the different harvest times,' their grandmother
continues, 'when we worked with the men in the fields. The girls
who brought the food which we ate under the olive trees . . . . And
what weddings we had in those days, they lasted several days and
nights. All the women wore their embroidered dresses, their gold
jewellery, their coin necklaces . . . and we danced . . . .'

'But Palestine was very unsettled,' Grandfather interrupts
in a dry, detached way, turning his beads between his fingers:

> After the English acquired their mandate over Palestine in
> the early 1920s, we began to feel that the Jews were our
> enemies, although we had been friends with the Jews for
> centuries, lived as their neighbours. . . . The English allowed
> more and more European Jews to move to Palestine. These
> European Jews bought up land and boycotted us, the Palesti-
> nians. They wanted to build their own state, and called them-
> selves Zionists! The English forced us to sell our harvests
> to their army and paid much less for it than we would have
> got at the market in Haifa. But in the 1930s it had gone too
> far! The farmers had to rebel against the English policies. I
> myself helped blow up their army barracks. We attacked
> their trains and bombed their cars.

The revolt began in 1936 with a six month general strike in all
the villages and towns throughout Palestine in a protest against
the English support of Zionist immigration. In due course the
strike turned into a full-scale war of resistance against the British
who only defeated the revolt, with the aid of the Zionists, in
1939. By the time it had been crushed, 3,112 Palestinians had
been killed and 1,175 injured. Some 329 Zionists had also been

killed and 857 injured, whilst the British lost 135 dead and 386 injured. In addition, 5,679 Palestinians were arrested and 110 hanged by the British during these years (see Chronology).

Fatima Ghazal (the woman wearing a white headscarf) was killed on the battlefield near Lydda in 1936. The village women were mainly messengers, hiding and smuggling weapons to the fighting men. And they also engaged in passive resistance. The British usually took the bodies of Palestinian men who had been killed in the fighting to the nearest village, demanding that the women identify the bodies. But the women would not bat an eyelid — not even if their son or husband was among the dead. They knew that the English would take revenge by shooting all young men in the village.

'Yes, the British were our enemy,' the old lady agrees. 'My mother and I walked to Haifa to sell our gold bracelets and spent the money on weapons for my father and brothers.'

'Many women did that,' Mouna adds. 'The gold bracelets are the woman's own capital. It was a big thing to sell one's security in order to help the men defend the home country. By the way, even then there were women fighting with arms. Fatima Ghazal was our first woman martyr.'

Then she tells us about the demonstrations and about how large groups of women would shout slogans against Zionism and the British. She remembers a verse she had made up herself:

'Palestine, Palestine, the guns are aimed at you, to scatter your families!'

'Apart from that, I wasn't very active,' she murmurs modestly. 'But I can tell you what my friend Nazirah did. One morning when she was going to the brook, she saw a group of men in the olive grove. They were dressed as Arabs but there was something wrong about the way they were behaving. She hid behind a tree and heard them speaking in English. They were British soldiers on their way to our village to take our weapons! She stole back to the village and warned the men who were having a meeting in the mosque. They took the weapons away and hid them in the fields. When the British arrived, they couldn't find any weapons. How we laughed at them afterwards!'

'But we were crushed in the end by the British, they forbade us to carry weapons,' the old man says heavily, leaning his head in his hands. 'We were not even allowed to fight on the side of the British against the Nazis in Africa. The Jews were, they had their own contingent in the British Army there! And the Jews smuggled weapons to Palestine.'

In 1939 the Second World War broke out. To prevent the Arabs turning to Germany for help, the British tried to stop Jewish immigration to Palestine. The Zionists then openly rebelled, in their turn, against the British. Meanwhile, skirmishes between Zionists and Palestinians continued. The situation eventually became untenable for Britain who turned over responsibility for Palestine to the UN in 1946. On 27 November 1947, the UN divided Palestine into two parts, one for Arabs and one for Jews. The Palestinians rejected the Partition Plan, and demonstrations and protests broke out all over the Arab world. The Zionists introduced psychological warfare in Palestine in order to terrify the population into leaving.

'By Allah, we just couldn't believe that the Zionists wanted to chase us away!' Grandmother exclaims with a sweeping gesture. The children's eyes are large and round, and the room is very quiet. We hear a car passing outside. 'No, we really didn't,' she repeats to herself. 'How could they possibly? we thought.'

It was relatively peaceful in that part of Galilee where the children's grandparents had lived. But still they increasingly heard rumours about the activities of the Zionists in other parts of the country in the 1940s. They heard of Zionist bomb attempts, attacks and murders, and had reports of growing numbers of Jews entering Palestine.

*When the UN presented their Partition Plan in 1947, Muslim and Christian
Palestinian women demonstrated in Jerusalem. The Muslim women wore
black veils. But, as early as 1920, women had been demonstrating against
Great Britain's support for the formation of a national home for Jews in
Palestine. In 1921 the first Palestine Women's Association was formed and
in 1929 its first congress was held with 300 delegates from all over the
country. The Palestinian women then demanded that a stop be put to the
growing Zionist immigration. They protested against the fact that Arabs
were taken prisoner and oppressed under the British mandate. The protests
and demonstrations continued throughout the 1930s.*

I understood it all one day at the market in Haifa. The
horrible truth was suddenly clear to me! The Zionists *were*
being serious! That day, in Haifa, was a shock . . . . A gang of
Zionists drove up in a car and threw a bomb in amongst the
stands. The bomb exploded, people screamed and ran in all
directions, blood squirting from their bodies, pieces of
human flesh stuck to the walls. Water gushed from blasted
water-mains . . . the children were petrified. They would

they would never go to Haifa after that, Mouna's grandmother recollected.

Since that day things have grown worse and worse, she concludes.

The room is completely still. The only sound is the clicking of
Grandfather's beads, as he lets one bead after another fall slowly
between his fingers. 'People began to talk about fleeing rather than
dying! Oh my God . . . it was after Deir Yassin, they called out the
terrible news from the minaret . . . .'

On 9 April 1948, 247 men, women and children were killed in
the village of Deir Yassin outside Jerusalem. Behind the massacre
were the Zionist terrorist groups — the Stern Gang and Irgun,
the latter led by Israel's present Prime Minister, Menachem Begin,
who remarked: 'The massacre was not only justified, it was
necessary; without the victory at Deir Yassin there would never
have been an Israeli state.' The massacre set an example and was
the touchpoint of the Palestinian exodus. Several similar massacres
were carried out in other villages during the month of April.
Before that date some 30,000 Palestinians had fled; then they
were seen as upper-class and wealthy middle-class traitors by the
Palestinians in the villages. But after Deir Yassin and during the
following months, some 800,000 Palestinians fled and the Zionists
were ecstatic over the 'country without people'!

'They proclaimed their state on 14 May 1948, and the war
began,' Grandmother continues. 'Not only did they take what the
UN had granted them, they also took our towns . . . Haifa and
Akka. . . but we stayed . . . Oh my God. . . .' Her small body
shivers. 'One morning in late May we were working in the fields
as usual . . . when bullets suddenly started to explode around
us. The Zionists had arrived! They had been hiding outside
the village overnight. We ran home, with bullets flying past
us, to get our weapons and to ensure that the children were
safe. We were completely unprepared for an attack on our area
. . . but they were determined to have everything!

She describes how the women took the children to a safe place
in the mosque. Some 150 people were packed together in the two
small rooms. The men defended the village and each time the
firing increased, the children screamed for their fathers. The old
people prayed to Allah. Eventually the Zionists retired, but
returned with a much larger force a few days later.

'We were fighting them entirely on our own,' Grandfather
explains, demonstrating with his hands how he had held his gun.

We had 60 old-fashioned guns and very little ammunition. We couldn't manage alone. We expected the Arab armies to come . . . but they didn't, they let us down! We fended off the Zionists twice, but on the last occasion we couldn't hold out. We ran out of ammunition. The Arab armies still had not arrived. We had no choice. We had to flee.'

'And we left very quickly,' the old woman continues. She gets up and walks around the room as she picks up the story. 'They were firing at us all the time. They blocked the roads and left only the fields north towards Lebanon open. Our mare lay shot on the ground, so we could only take a few things. We had to carry the youngest children and I was seven months pregnant. It was gruelling!'

They remember whole villages fleeing, and that at times there were long columns on the roads. They remember the Zionists firing after them to force them on and prevent them from stopping. They had no food and no water.

'I have never been more thirsty,' Grandmother exclaims, sitting down. 'People collapsed with exhaustion. I remember an old man who sat down by the verge. "I'd rather be killed by the Zionists than flee with my tail between my legs." he said. I shall never forget him, I saw a bullet hit his body and then he collapsed.'

For two days they walked without stopping before they finally reached Lebanon. Grandmother recalls how the prickly mountain plants tore their clothes and skin and how it was a whole month before she had removed the last thorn. 'We believed we would soon return,' her husband says slowly. 'We had only left the village for a short period, or so we thought; we had even taken the key to the house.' He pointed to a rusty old key hanging on the wall above Mouna.

'The Arab armies promised they would liberate Palestine. So we waited and yearned . . . . Some months passed, a year, and now, over thirty years have elapsed! . . . We have long since stopped believing in other people's promises. . . .'

He is interrupted by the crackling of the minaret loudspeaker where a voice is announcing:

A message to the inhabitants of the Rashidiyeh camp!
    The People's Committee wants to remind everyone that it is no longer permitted to draw water from the mains without special permission!
    We also remind our brothers and sisters that drinking

alcohol is unhealthy. Alcohol is only evil, destroying your body as well as your soul, and harms the cause of the Revolution!

The People's Committee also wants to remind everyone that it is strictly forbidden to use weapons without a reason! *Thawra Haata Naasr* — Revolution to Victory!

Immediately after this message a machine gun is fired nearby.

When the State of Israel was proclaimed in 1948, the Western press was full of congratulations. There was no mention of the 800,000 Palestinians fleeing from their homes.

Everybody laughs and the serious mood changes. Um Immad asks her daughter Josra to prepare some coffee. But their grandfather does not smile; staring silently at the floor, he takes out his tobacco bag and searches through his pockets for paper. While he was talking, his face had grown sombre and it is difficult to tell whether he feels grief or anger. 'Pardon the tears and harsh words of an old man,' he exclaims in a trembling voice. 'It's very

51

difficult, I don't want to remember those days. It was an evil time and every day was just a matter of survival . . . nothing else. We felt powerless . . . and the shame . . . .'

When they were first in Lebanon they lived under a large tree, and slept on the ground. In due course they found a deserted old house in the mountains and moved into it. Three years later, they were moved by the Lebanese authorities to the Al Bass camp in Sour because they didn't want any Palestinians so near the border. The Al Bass camp was built up by Palestinians with material from UNRWA. Conditions were terrible, the camp was unhealthy and many of the inhabitants contracted malaria. Sixteen years later, some Lebanese archaeologists ordered Um Immad's family to move again. The explanation they gave was that Roman remains had been found under their house.

'And so we came to Rashidiyeh,' his wife completes their story, her eyes on the key hanging on the wall over Mouna's head.

9. 'Having Only Two Children Ought To Be Forbidden'

The women try to get most of the housework done in the morning. During the afternoon they like to visit each other. Life in the camp depends on this network of social visits, which are obligatory, particularly if someone has died. But they are also made in connection with births, engagements, weddings, and if someone has been promoted, taken an exam, or has returned after a long absence. If someone is ill, the women visit in a group. A sick person is never alone.

It is mainly the women's responsibility to maintain social relations and thus preserve the close-knit exiled community. It is a community where family means a lot, as in the rest of the Arab world. Mouna explains with a sigh:

> If I don't visit my relations every day, they think something's the matter. It can even lead to conflicts between related families. We women have an almost diplomatic function, we hold the peace and mediate in sensitive situations. Of course, the men rule and decide for us. 'It's tradition', they say, and the Koran proclaims that man is woman's master. But the women do the work. The men play an insignificant role, they are out all day long! Many women have no husband. Look at all our widows. If the husband is dead, the eldest son takes over responsibility, but he in turn may be working far from home, perhaps in the guerrilla forces or abroad. Those women carry all the responsibility themselves.

We visit Um Ali in the house opposite with Mouna and Um Immad. Um Ali is not a relation but she is a neighbour and has recently become a grandmother. Her daughter-in-law Samiah has just come back from hospital after having had her first baby. Her other children will probably be born at home, helped by experienced women or a trained midwife.

Samiah blushes and gives us a weak smile from where she's lying on a couch in Um Ali's sitting-room. The afternoon sun streams between the blue-green shutters. The room is full of visitors, women talking eagerly to each other and children crowding in the doorway leading to the courtyard. Samiah gently strokes her new green nylon nightgown, fingering the lace on her swollen, milk-filled bosom. The nightgown is a gift, just like the paper flower arrangements and the chocolates in gold wrappings which are offered to us. We drink Arab coffee brought in by one of Um Ali's daughters.

The new-born baby boy is being passed from one woman to another like a little parcel. He is tightly wrapped and wears a blazing white shirt. The minute he gives a squeak, he is rocked until he's silent.

'*Helweh! Helweh kitir!*'. — He's so beautiful! So beautiful! the women exclaim. 'How fortunate that it was a boy! God be praised,' Um Immad says, pinching his cheek.

'Now Samiah will be saved from the silence following the birth of a daughter,' Mouna explains, putting down the little cup with coffee dregs at the bottom. 'Girls are burdens, people say, a daughter only gives financial problems, but a son means the birth of a new family which will preserve the family name."Homes with many daughters are very poor homes" is another saying. You know, a son helps his parents with money through his work, and he takes on financial responsibility for the parents when they grow old.'

Mouna translates for Um Ali and the other women, who nod, smiling. Oh yes, that's right! 'Samiah,' Um Ali exclaims, 'you're not Samiah any more, you're Um Mohammed, your son will be called Mohammed after the Prophet and his grandfather!'

Samiah smiles proudly as she takes over her son. Now the girl has become a woman and is included in the circle of mothers. The more children she has, the more authority will she have. Besides, she managed to have her first child within a year of her marriage. If she had taken any longer, people would have been wondering. Newly-wed girls are under a lot of pressure to get pregnant immediately. There is no fear of pregnancy here, rather the opposite. A barren woman has a low status. Her husband can repudiate her and she will then be forced to return to her old home with no future. Even if her husband chooses to keep her, he is permitted to take on another wife who can bear his children. Equally, a man who turns out to be sterile is disgraced for life and his wife has the right to leave him.

One of Um Ali's boys comes running in, quite breathless. He has something to tell her. The children are always the messengers, reporting to the adults what goes on in the alley. 'Um Leila is coming!' Um Leila is the woman activist whom we met in Beirut. We know that she's a longstanding friend of Um Ali's.

When Um Leila enters the room, Um Ali gets up and covers her in kisses and greetings. They sit down, their arms around each other. The other women stop talking and watch them. Um Leila has travelled from Beirut to discuss the day nursery with Mouna.

'Each time I visit Um Ali, she's carrying a new baby. Each time she promises that it will be her last. Now she's expecting her seventeenth,' Um Leila says, patting Um Ali's tummy with a laugh.

'Having only two children ought to be forbidden,' Um Ali replies jokingly.

'A disgrace! You need at least five boys and five girls. Um Leila, your husband is a cad not to demand a son from you!' Um Leila giggles in delight. She has chosen to have only two children, both of whom are girls. Also, she calls herself Um Leila after the eldest girl, and this is a great provocation to the camp women. It's a deliberate strategy to start discussions about sex roles and child-bearing, and she always succeeds.

'I'm thirty-six,' Um Ali says proudly, jerking her head. 'I'm young! I can still have children!' The women in the room nod, adjusting their headscarfs. A few are breast-feeding their children without inhibition. The minute a child makes a noise, the breast is offered. 'She's not lazy, Um Leila, she's working herself to death for the Revolution,' Um Ali says approvingly. 'But she could easily manage many children and still work. Look at me, I work for the Revolution in spite of all my children.' She points to Yasser Arafat on the wall over the Fatah shield — the Fatah emblem of two crossed machine guns over Palestine.

Um Ali washes and irons uniforms for the soldiers, and helps with practical matters for the Women's Association. She was one of those who insisted on the building of an air-raid shelter in Rashidiyeh. She is known to be a very wise woman and many people visit her to ask for advice.

During the whole of the conversation children are coming up to her, she helps one pull up his trousers, she comforts another who has fallen and hurt himself. We are impressed by these strong,

upright women who radiate a special kind of security where they sit on the chairs around the room with children on their laps, these are middle-aged women whose natural condition is pregnancy, and whose bodies are marked both by this and by the heavy work they do every day. We admire their endurance and ask ourselves where they get their strength. However their anxiety and fatigue has to find expression somehow, and though they love their children, it is they who are often rebuked and struck.

'I've been told that in the West you don't have so many children,' Um Ali says. 'But you don't have our problem. We need our children. Our children are our future, our hope! We have so many martyrs, so many who die in the war. You can see how the Zionists' weapons can so easily kill us!'

She points to the heavy shell case placed on the table, filled with plastic carnations, and she points to the cupboard where a row of shell cases, painted in pastel colours, are displayed on a shelf. We've seen the same thing in many homes. 'Didn't you hear what happened the other day? A little boy playing in the field where they are accustomed to play, died, because he found an Israeli grenade in the sand. It had been there for nine months, ever since the invasion last March. It exploded in his hand. Oh my God, what grief for his mother, what tremendous grief for our people!' Um Ali's voice breaks and her eyes fill with tears. The women put their hands in front of their eyes, rocking back and forth. The emotions are so strong in the room, death is so close, and the pain shows as deep furrows in the women's faces.

'I have a friend from Tal al Zaatar,' Um Abdullah says with her eyes on the shell cases on the shelf. 'Her sister persuaded her to go on the Pill after her sixth child. But look what happened to her! Five of her children were killed in Tal al Zaatar. "You and your bright ideas!" she shouted at her sister. "Now I have only one child left, and a girl! My husband was killed, too. How shall I ever get more children? Where is my security now? If only I had had more children!"'

The older women frequently say that 'The Revolution needs children' and 'The Israelis bomb our children', but at the same time, they complain about being 'men factories', made only to bear boys. We learn also that it is religion which makes women bear so many children, and poverty that forces them to have children as a social insurance for the future.

There are many reasons, and constant discussions as to how many children a woman should have, but it's certain that the

Fragmentation bombs dropped by Israeli planes over Rashidiyeh. The fragmentation bombs are made in the US and given to Israel. On each bomb is a label: 'Warranty' — a guarantee that the bomb is thoroughly effective. These bombs are blind shells, each one filled with 717 separate bullets.

that the younger women do not want to have as many as their mothers. 'I'm twenty-four,' says Um Ahmed who lives further down the alley. 'I've had four children and that's enough! Many of my contemporaries have the same view.'

'That's true,' Um Leila says to us:

> Not only the war claims its victims, many small children die of diseases. Um Ali has had sixteen children, but only ten of them are alive. We try to convince those women whose men make very little money that too many children is expensive. We say that the Revolution wants quality, not quantity! We're not very successful, but a woman who used to aim at twelve children may choose now to have only six. It's a slow progress, but we can't expect everything at once. Many more women are now going on the Pill, but they often keep this a secret from their husband and mother-in-law. Abortions are very unusual, although they do happen. The women make themselves miscarry by putting a heavy pestle and mortar

A charge in each bomb makes it burst into hundreds of sharp little metal fragments which spread over an area of 500 square metres with a violent force. Israel claim that their fragmentation bombs are used in self-defence.

59

on their stomach or drinking herbal mixtures which have the same effect. The men, of course, never know anything about it.

Um Ali suddenly interrupts us. It's difficult to keep the thread when there are so many people together. They all talk a lot at the same time. 'I bring up my children to be revolutionaries,' she says. 'I tell them about Palestine. I explain how unfairly my people have been treated. I send my children, both boys and girls, to *Ashbal* and *Zahrat.*' *Ashbal* means 'the lion cubs' and *zahrat* 'the flowers'. There children, up to the age of fifteen, are given military training. They learn how to handle a machine gun and receive physical training. At the same time they learn about Palestine's history, and they act and sing.

Um Ali goes to the cupboard, unlocks it, rummages for a while and eventually takes out a parcel wrapped in plastic with a ribbon tied round it. She carefully unties the ribbon and produces a bunch of well-thumbed pictures. She finds a blurred colour photo of a young boy dressed in his best clothes.

'This is my son Assad! He's sixteen and he's in the guerrilla forces!'

From the courtyard outside, we suddenly hear a steady thumping rhythm with a quickening beat. Children's voices shout and laugh. Um Immad rises, looks out of the open window and smiles. Her daughter Josra is sitting on a stool, drumming intently on a plastic water-can turned upside down, and some other girls dance next to her, wriggling their little girls' bodies in an Arab belly-dance, moving their hips softly and gently and waving slowly with extended arms. Josra starts to sing a popular song about a Bedouin camp finally getting electricity.

'Ya Josra,' Um Ali shouts, putting down the picture of her son. 'Sing the song about us not allowing the aeroplanes to frighten us!' 'Yes,' the other children in the courtyard scream. 'Sing the aeroplane song!' Josra changes the beat and goes on singing. The women in the room leave their seats and stand crowded together at the window and around the door. They clap their hands, yelling and encouraging the children to go on singing. Two girls with their hair smeared with henna, school-books in their hands, look in from the alley and join in the singing.

But Um Abdullah stays sitting on the bed with a little boy whose eye is infected. She has put her hand lightly on his head and is mumbling verses from the Koran with half-closed eyes, yawning.

Um Abdullah often intervenes and tries to cure illness with Allah's help. The boy sits stiffly on the bed, his head bent, whilst he glances yearningly towards the courtyard.

10. Maternal Love

Khaled is a man with kind serious eyes and a stubbly chin. When he joined Fatah, one of his first tasks was to work in the camp militia in Rashidiyeh and during this time he made friends with Mouna and became a frequent visitor in Um Immad's house. Thirty-two years ago he was born in Jenin in Palestine. When Israel was founded, the family fled to Jordan. In 1966 Khaled and his older brother went to live in West Germany, where Khaled went to university. There he met Germans who were deeply involved in the student revolts of the late 1960s.

He became active in the Palestinian liberation struggle while his brother concentrated solely on getting a job and starting a new life, so that he could forget his old one. Khaled was registered by the police as a Palestinian activist. He was then ordered to leave the country, together with 249 other Palestinians, after the Palestinian attack on the Israeli team at the Olympic Games in Munich in 1972, although he had had nothing to do with the attempt. He could not return to Jordan, because the Palestinian liberation groups had all been forced to leave the country the year before. So, he went to Beirut where he soon joined the guerrillas. He has not seen his family in Jordan even once in the past ten years.

In spite of the sense of comradeship in the movement, he missed his friends in West Germany. So, in February 1978, after six years' absence, he got into West Germany illegally to see his friends and brother. It was then that he found out that his mother had died. 'You know,' he says gently, 'I loved my mother above everything else. My brother and I were walking in the street in Berlin when he told me that my mother had died eight months previously. He had had a letter from Jordan . . . and I knew nothing! I broke down completely, crying desperately in the middle of the street . . . . It was the blackest day of my life.' Khaled rubs his eyes. When he talks about his mother, he goes from joy to sorrow. Every word he speaks about her has a glow about it. 'She was a strong woman. So strong! She fought and struggled and was the one who kept the family going. We were poor, not starving, but we often went to bed hungry.'

During the wheat harvest, his mother would go out to the fields to gather harvest waste, picking out the wheat ears to make bread for the children. She took any casual jobs she could get, working in the fields all year round, even during Ramadan, the month of fasting, when she was not allowed food while the sun was up. At the same time she kept the home clean and tidy, mended the children's clothes, cooked, washed up . . . everything! The heavy work broke her down physically, she had terrible pains in her joints but she still went on working. And, as Khaled tells us:

> She taught me what resistance really means. A mother is the children's first teacher, and my mother made me understand how important the Revolution is. She always talked about Palestine! She said it was our *duty* to support the Revolution and fight to return to Palestine! She was the most important person in my life. When my brother told me about my mother's death, I felt the hate growing inside me. My brother is happy in Germany, he has forgotten Palestine and doesn't want to know about the liberation struggle . . . but my mother gave her life to it. I was crying there in the street, in front of all those Germans. I cried because my brother had let our mother down! . . . I couldn't stay with him. In a daze I went to my German friends. Of course, they felt sorry for me but they couldn't understand the depth of my grief. They asked me why I hadn't been to see her in all those years. *But I couldn't!*

Khaled is screaming: '*I couldn't*. If I had gone to see her in Jordan, the authorities would have thrown me into prison! There's nothing I would rather have done than be with her on her death-bed . . . .'

When we discuss maternal love with Palestinian men, they open up and their emotions well up, without restraint. Their steely masculine facade disappears and they become humble. When we mentioned to a Palestinian that many men in the West lose contact or break away from their parents as they grow up, he just dismissed it with a wave. 'Impossible here,' he exclaimed. 'Nothing is as strong as the ties between mother and child. The child has been inside the mother's body, it is and remains part of her.'

Sabha is an old woman.
Sixty years old . . .
Her heart is green, green, green.
Like an old tree —
as old as the earth.

Her son . . .
. . . will soon be nine.
But he knows how to throw stones!
And he knows how to shout:
Oh, Palestine!

His mother shouted as they knocked him down:
Leave my son alone!
Leave my son alone!
Isn't it enough that you've killed his father and brother?

But the devil only smiled,
and told her:
Listen, old woman!
We'll slaughter all who don't obey.

But then the mother produced a knife,
and before he raised his hand
she sank it deep into his heart.

Abu Sadek Husseini
(One of the most beloved poets
among the exiled Palestinians, the
author of the most popular
fighting songs of the liberation
movement.)

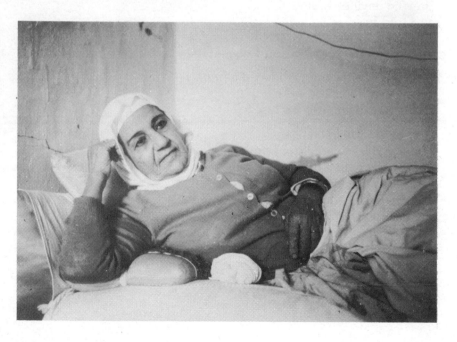

Many older women have blue tattoos on their faces. Girls used to be tattooed at the age of ten, but this tradition has now died out.

11. 'Knowledge Is A Strong Weapon'

Mouna's younger sister, Josra, who is ten years old, is sitting in the gateway watching her younger brothers and sisters, who are playing with sticks in the gully. Um Immad has forbidden them to do this but Josra does no notice, she is deeply absorbed in a book on mathematics. Um Immad turns into the alley and observes the children, but instead of scolding Josra, she drives the children into the courtyard. Josra takes a deep breath and apologizes.

'*Malesh*,' Um Immad replies — it's all right. 'You read your book!' Um Immad is proud of the fact that Josra is studying, and like other Palestinians she is very concerned that her children get educated. The Palestinians are one of the best-educated nations in the Middle East, including Israel. 'I want to be an electrical engineer,' Josra says. 'Then I could repair the whole electricity network here in Rashidiyeh. Now it breaks down almost every day. And when we go back to Palestine, I can help build up the country again.'

'Knowledge is a strong weapon,' Mouna explains. 'Before the Revolution, education was our only weapon with which to fight poverty and unemployment. A good education means the possibility of a good job and of making a contribution towards the upkeep of the family. It's still the same. We can't be an uneducated people when we liberate Palestine, otherwise we shall just be exploited as cheap labour by the Israelis who remain behind, and we won't be able to develop our country.'

Everywhere in the camps we see children carrying books and girls doing their homework at the same time as the housework. The boys are given more freedom to study. The children are forced to learn to concentrate in the crowded homes where small children are playing, the radio is on, and a constant stream of visitors walk in and out. To find peace to study, Josra goes onto the roof terrace where she paces back and forth reading aloud from the open textbook.

The war is another, far more serious cause of disturbance, and schooling in Rashidiyeh is totally disrupted during an Israeli bombardment. The school closes and many families flee north. Schools in the Beirut camps become temporary homes for the refugees from the south, and in turn those schoolchildren have their education disrupted. It's a vicious circle which affects many Palestinian schoolchildren and prevents continuous schooling. The Rashidiyeh school has been hit several times by Israeli shells, bombs and rockets.

The schools in the camps work a shift system to give all children a chance to attend. After many long disruptions, there are now three shifts a day to make up for the time that has been lost. Higher education has also been hit by the war. Education lies dormant for long periods at a time and the Beirut universities have been forced to close on several occasions since the Civil War started in 1975. There are still Palestinian refugee children who don't go to school but today it is an exception to keep girls of Josra's age at home. The children start in the UN schools at the age of six or seven, and the girls and boys are segregated so that girls can't be kept at home because their mothers think they see too many boys at school.

No real distinctions are made until the students reach university level. Many families still feel that it is more important to give their sons a good education. University education costs money, but the camp families are poor and if money is to be spent on it, their sons are given priority since it is they who will have to support a family. Many parents also dislike the fact that their daughters will have to study and live in Beirut beyond the surveillance of the family, although this is now changing. Nevertheless, most camp women over thirty are still illiterate. It's amongst the younger women that the difference can be seen most clearly. 'I can neither read nor write,' Um Immad tells us. 'But my youngest sister who is twenty is now studying in Iraq. She is training to be a doctor! In my days it was inconceivable for a farmer's daughter to become a doctor! "Why do you want your daughter to be able to write?" people used to ask. "So she can write love letters?" Mouna explains:

Since the Revolution more and more camp women have received the chance of further education. The Women's

69

Union receives grants from the Socialist countries so
that the families can afford to send them there. Still, even
that is not always enough. It's a pity. On one occasion we
were given twenty university grants from the Soviet Women's
Association but we could only find sixteen girls willing to go.
Many girls take the view that: 'If I go to university, I won't
finish my studies until I'm twenty-three or twenty-four.
Then it will be difficult to find a husband.' Most men in the
camps like to marry young girls of sixteen or seventeen. If
a woman is over twenty and still without a husband, her
chances of ever finding one diminish. Besides, there are few
men who want to marry a girl who is better educated than
themselves. In the camp community the man should have the
education and the responsibility for the family. An educated
woman would threaten his traditional male role. So I shall
probably never marry.

*Successful pupils are encouraged and the children study to learn. The school
premises are worn down and cramped.*

The last remark she makes with a grimace. Then she starts laughing.

In the midst of the PLO area in Beirut are several SAMED factories. This woman works with hosiery.

Some 7% only of the camp women work outside the home. Uneducated Palestinian camp women are sought after by Lebanese employers; it pays to employ a Palestinian woman, because the employer bears no responsibility and does not have to pay her as much as he does a Palestinian man. Palestinians in turn are paid less than the Lebanese for doing the same job. The women from the Beirut camps — usually widows or divorcees — usually work as cleaners of public premises. Many of them used to work in the factories situated in East or North Beirut, but at the end of the Civil War these factories fell within the area controlled by the Lebanese right wing and no Palestinian would enter there. Many

women from the camps around Sour work for Lebanese land-
owners, in their fields and orchards.

When the PLO took over the camps and increased its activities
in Lebanon, women were employed in the Palestinian Red
Crescent — the PLO health organization. Over 60% of the workers
there are women. Others work in SAMED — the Movement of
Martyr Sons. SAMED runs several factories and workshops
manufacturing leather goods, toys, Palestinian crafts, textiles and
military clothes etc. About 70% of the workers are women. As for
women with higher education, they can find jobs in the many PLO
offices and institutions in Beirut. In addition, the Marxist
commando groups, the Popular Front and the Democratic Front,
run their own clinics, embroidery workshops, day nurseries and
courses which employ women. But the women in the various
commando groups all work together in the PLO Women's
Association. They want to co-ordinate the different projects —
day nurseries and training courses — but this is not very well
received by the men in their respective organizations.

The official aim of the PLO Women's Association is to make the
Palestinian woman more aware of her situation and to mobilize
her in the liberation struggle. Most of the Association activities
take place in the camps. Mouna tells us:

> Our resources are very limited, so we can only concentrate
> on a few projects in each camp. First of all, we must make
> contact with the women and gain their confidence. We
> meet them at wedding celebrations, funerals and other
> occasions when they are all together. We also go around
> knocking on doors and inviting them to an initial meeting
> to discuss what they themselves consider to be most
> important. The first time they talk a lot about their personal
> problems, the words come pouring out, they want to talk
> about problems with their children, husband or neighbours.
> At that stage we do not discuss politics, we deal with
> practical issues, for example, the kind of improvements they
> would like to see happen in the camp. In Rashidiyeh the
> women wanted more shelters and water-conduits, for
> instance, but it's different in each camp. We discuss the
> problems and in due course we form committees to influence
> the camp management. It's important to show the women

that we can do something. And, eventually, when we have
their confidence, we present suggestions for various projects,
sewing classes, literacy classes, day nurseries . . . the women
choose for themselves.

The most popular project, according to Mouna, is the day
nurseries, and secondly, the sewing classes. The older women
ought to go to literacy classes to learn to read and write, but they
are so busy with their homes and children that they feel it's
better to let the younger ones go to sewing classes in order to
learn an occupation. She goes on:

> In the day nurseries, boys and girls are together. Many of
> the boys' mothers were very upset by this, because they
> didn't want their sons to do the same things as the girls.
> When the mothers come to complain, they are making
> contact with us, and that's exactly what we want. Then we
> can start explaining to them that there is no difference
> between the things boys and girls can or ought to do. But
> while the day nurseries give us the best opportunities for
> contact, they are also very expensive. Each day nursery
> must have its own shelter. We must be able to guarantee the
> safety of the children in case the Israelis bomb us.
>
> The greatest problem of the Women's Union is the
> lack of continuity in its work. Each time the camps are
> bombed, the day nurseries are closed, the classes are inter-
> rupted, and it may be a long time before everything starts
> up again. Many activists disappear because they get married.
> They either join their husbands in other countries where the
> men have got work, or even if they stay their husbands
> forbid them to go on working. I can tell you about one of
> our activists. She was an untrained seamstress who had learnt
> to read and write. She worked well, with great enthusiasm,
> and we made her responsible for our sewing classes. Our
> newspaper took several pictures of her, and she happily cut
> out one of them and fixed it to the wall at home. It made her
> extremely happy. But when her husband came back and saw
> the picture, he was furious. 'So you are the man now and
> I'm the woman!' he shouted, tearing the picture to shreds. 'I
> forbid you to go back to that place! If you do, I'll divorce
> you!' We did everything to convince him that his conditions
> were absurd. But when our sister put the picture up again, he

نشرة
الاتحاد العام للمرأة الفلسطينية
تصدر عن اللجنة التنفيذية

العدد الثاني
شباط
١٩٧٦

تنظيمية ، سياسية ، ثقافية ، اجتماعية

فليبق الاصبع على الزناد

الحاكمة بشقيها المسلم والمسيحي ٠٠ مكرسا الاوضاع الطائفية بصورة أسوأ مما عرف لبنان من قبل ٠٠٠ اذ جعل الطائفية مدونة بعد ان كانت عرفا فقط ٠ وربما كانت الحسنة الوحيدة للميثاق الجديد والتي جاءت تراجعا من القوى الانعزالية لضغط ضربات الحركة

الرجعية والانعزالية تلقي بكل ثقلها من أجل ضرب الحركة الوطنية والتقدمية اللبنانية وعزل المقاومة الفلسطينية تمهيدا لتصفيتها ومن ثم العمل من أجل تنفيذ مؤامرة التصفية النهائية للقضية الفلسطينية ٠٠ عبر ادخال القضية برمتها ضمن مخطط التسوية ٠٠ ذلك ان الساحة اللبنانية قد بدأت تشكل

حين وقفت الجماهير اللبنانية ، لتعلــن رفضها للاستغلال والاحتكار والامتيـازات ، حين وقفت تقدم قوافل الشهداء من أجل بناء لبنان الجديد ٠٠ لبنان العربي ، لبنــان العدل والمساواة والديمقراطية الحقيقيــة المعبرة عن ارادة كل الجماهير ٠ حددت موقفا صريحا وواضحا ٠٠ وضعت

'Keep your finger on the trigger' ran a headline in the newspaper of the Women's Union. 'To organize the women's ability and strength is a foundation stone in the liberation struggle' says the slogan next to the Union's emblem. The Palestine Women's Union (GUPW — General. Union of Palestinian Women) was founded in 1965 in Jerusalem as a division of the PLO. The Union has branches in all Arab countries where Palestinians live: Lebanon, Syria, Egypt, Iraq, Kuwait. In Jordan and Israel they work underground. The Executive Committee of the Women's Union consists of women from Fatah (6), PFLP (2), DFLP (1), ALF (1), PFLP General Command (1), SAIKA (1) and one independent who is the Chairperson. Twelve out of 200 members of the PLO National Council are women. No woman is represented on the PLO Executive Committee.

took their children to his mother in Saida, forbade her to see them and divorced her! He simply told her to go, that's enough for a divorce, according to Muslim tradition. And he was a man who worked for the Revolution!

Mouna sighed. 'There are so many cases like this . . . but sometimes we manage to sort them out.'

She tells us about another women, Khadija, who works in a day nursery. She is a very good mother, has common sense and treats other children as her own. But the Women's Union had problems with her husband. He demanded that she leave her job, although the family needed her wages. They quarrelled each time Khadija went to work. She had to get up particularly early to make breakfast, wash her husband's clothes and clean the house before going to work. But she managed. When Mouna met

Khadija's husband some time ago, he said: 'Do you remember, Mouna, how opposed I was to Khadija going out to work? Well, now I respect her work, although she can't cope with everything at home as well.'

Day nursery children learn arithmetic, writing, and Arabic.

Mouna took us to a sewing class in Bourj al Shemaleh, a camp three kilometres north of Rashidiyeh. We walked through the maze of narrow winding lanes that ran around the houses and courtyards. It was uphill all the way until we finally stopped in front of a house painted yellow on the edge of the camp, overlooking a view of Sour and the Mediterranean.

When we entered about fifteen to twenty young women, mostly teenagers, were sitting around a large table folding long lengths of material. In a corner of the room hung a large Palestinian flag with a picture of Yasser Arafat pinned on to it. Beside one of the short walls were two treadle sewing machines and a dismantled

knitting machine. All the women greeted Mouna enthusiastically
and looked at us curiously whilst storing away the lengths of
material in a grey metal cupboard. 'Only two of the women on the
course are married,' Mouna said. This is always the way. It's the
unmarried women who have both the time and opportunity. When
they leave here, they can start sewing on commission at home, or
take jobs at the SAMED factory in the camp. It may be their first
step towards financial independence.'

Mouna went up to a notice-board. Among the hand-written
notes in Arabic was a caricature of Israel's Prime Minister Begin
and Egypt's President Sadat embracing, while in the background
the US President Carter blesses them. 'This drawing was done by
some of the girls,' Mouna tells us eagerly, 'and on it one of them
has written that peace negotiations between Egypt and Israel
are pointless so long as they exclude the Palestinians. It is, after
all, our country they are discussing! We encourage the girls to talk
about issues which are developing in the Middle East —
imperialism, women's lib, other political and social issues —
topics they don't usually have a chance to discuss. If you don't
mind, I'm going to take advantage of your visit,' she continues and
claps her hands.

The girls stop talking and listen as Mouna tells them who we
are and that we're from Sweden. Does anyone want to ask
questions? Everyone does, and we are soon crammed together on
chairs in a corner of the room, while the questions rain over us:
What do Swedish people think of Palestinians? What do the
Swedish people think about the Palestinian liberation struggle?
What do Swedes know about the refugee camps. Do they know
that the Israelis bomb the camps? What do Swedes think of
Zionists? Of Israel?

We have often heard these questions, from young and old, men
and women. In response we say that most Swedes know little
of the Palestinians and their life. They recall the extermination of
the Jews in Germany and therefore prefer to support Israel. One
girl reacts immediately to this. 'But it's *not our fault* that Hitler
exterminated Jews! That happened in Europe! Why should the
Palestinians be punished for that?'

The women heatedly discuss something amongst themselves.
Some of them ask questions about Sweden: Is Sweden at war?
Another question we've become accustomed to. No, we reply,
Sweden has not been involved in a war for over 160 years. Today
it's a so-called neutral country. The women express amazement,

they don't believe that such a situation can exist anywhere in the world. Can it really be true?

'Are the Swedish people rich or poor? Do they have as many children as we do in Palestine?' We explain that there are both rich and poor in Sweden but that no one starves. We explain about our social services and tell them that most Swedish families have only two children, that the family means less than it does in Palestine, and that many Swedes feel lonely . . . .

'Don't Swedes like children? Doesn't the family look after those who are lonely? I feel sorry for the Swedes,' is the immediate response to our words. 'Do Swedish women work or do they stay at home?' We tell them that many more women work outside the home than in the Middle East and that there are some fathers who stay at home and look after the children while their wives go to work, although it's still not common practice. We tell them that the Swedish Government has launched an advertising campaign that includes a poster showing a man holding a little child in his arms, which announces that fathers are entitled to paid leave to look after their children. The women gape, laugh and talk simultaneously. 'If someone were to put up such a poster next to our posters of martyrs, he would be shot,' one girl giggles. 'Men are needed for fighting.'

The girls want to know what Sweden looks like, if it's hot, if there's industry there. We explain that Sweden is highly industrialized, and that the winters are cold and accompanied by snow, and that parts of the Baltic Sea freeze . . . 'The sea freezes?' one girls says, reflecting, 'What if the Mediterranean froze! Then we could walk on the sea to Palestine!'

12. How Jamilah Learnt to Walk

In our alley there's a door which is always locked in the mornings. That's where Um Fahdi lives with her five children. Um Fahdi is thirty-two and one of the many widows in Rashidiyeh. She supports her children alone, and therefore she has been offered the job of cook at a guerrilla base not far from the camp. The policy of the liberation movement is to offer work rather than money to those who need support.

Um Fahdi is therefore away all day, leaving early in the morning and returning home at dusk. Only in the evenings and on Sunday, her day off, can the family get together. Her three older children go to school, while the younger two have got places in the Women's Union day nursery a few streets away. The children return home in the afternoon and the two older boys disappear to the training field and club-house of the Pioneers. The Pioneers is a youth movement for children between eight and twelve, run by the Popular Front, one of the Marxist groups in the PLO, Rim, the eldest daughter, collects her younger brother and sister from the day nursery. She cleans the house, washes up, cooks, does the laundry and looks after the younger ones until her mother comes home.

Um Abdullah, their neighbour, frequently pops in to help Rim. She has become a second mother to the children and has taught Rim many of the skills she now needs and will need when she gets married and has her own household to run.

Um Fahdi lost her husband in 1976. The family then lived in Tal al Zaatar, the large refugee camp in East Beirut, in the middle of the right wing's territory. Throughout the Civil War, Tal al Zaatar was besieged by the Lebanese right wing. Her husband, Abu Fahdi, was shot dead by a sniper one morning when he tried to get to the barricades. Over 3,000 Palestinians were killed during the siege, which lasted for more than seventeen months. During the final 53 days the camp was hit by 60,000 shells. At last the population of Tal al Zaatar capitulated and the survivors were given safe-conduct on 12 August 1976.

Um Fahdi is an energetic, optimistic woman. Her short curly hair keeps falling into her eyes, and two gold teeth glitter when she laughs. But she is marked for life by the experiences in Tal al Zaatar, and her eyes are melancholy. Many people here have such eyes, eyes that have seen and lived through immense suffering and humiliation. She has pains in her stomach which are sometimes so bad as to contort her face. She often touches the right side of her body, just beneath her lung. 'Since Tal al Zaatar I find it difficult to sleep,' Um Fahdi says in a hoarse voice. 'I lie awake at night listening to the silence, without even a radio . . . staring at the ceiling in the dark . . . thinking . . . trying to sleep, but it's impossible. Not until two or three in the morning . . . and then I have to get up at six.'

We're sitting on a rickety iron bed in Um Fahdi's house while she and the children are sitting on the floor, trying to make tea. But the electric ring on their one hot plate is broken. For the current to go through it, the ring has to be held together. Un Fahdi puts a knife against it, the ring sparks and crackles and she is given an electric shock which makes her jump. She laughs, tries again and eventually succeeds. But she has received a small charge and when she touches her eldest son Fahdi, he is also given a shock. However he laughs happily, takes the knife and gives his little brother a shock, and soon all the children have gathered around the plate and play at giving each other shocks. It is extremely dangerous, but in this camp where nothing works properly, dangers are turned into games. Burns, especially of children, are the most common injury.

'We don't have a lot here,' Um Fahdi says, nodding towards the broken hot plate. 'We lost everything in Tal al Zaatar. Everything! The Movement has helped us get some mattresses and blankets. The utensils we were given were plastic. When I get my next wages, I shall buy some spoons and a small gas stove.'

Um Fahdi lost 67 out of her 86 relations in Tal al Zaatar. Most of them died at the same time in a cellar they used as a shelter. The block of flats above it collapsed under heavy firing from the right-wing artillery and 650 people were crushed to death. 'The

block was built in columns,' she explains. 'The Fascists shot down
the columns, one after another. There was only one way out, so
they all gathered in the middle of the room. But the roof collapsed
in the centre. Only one child survived, she was standing in the
doorway . . . . '

Um Fahdi stares into the distance, her eyes shining with tears.
At that moment the electricity goes out and the room is plunged
into darkness. Our glowing cigarettes gleam. Um Fahdi swears
under her breath and asks Rim to charge the fuse in the bedroom.
The hot plate overloads the system and blows the fuse in this way
several times during the evening. But the electricity soon returns
and Fahdi and Rim help each other with their homework while
the younger children pinch one another, teasing and pushing,
whispering and giggling. Um Fahdi tells the children to go to bed.
She watches the naughtiness in the bedroom in silence and smiles
softly at her four-year-old daughter Jamilah jumping up and down
on a mattress. 'I'll tell you how Jamilah learnt to walk,' she says.
'It was during the siege and Jamilah was little more than a year
old. One evening two shells hit our house, one hit the wall and the
other the ceiling! We rushed to the kitchen for shelter and in the

confusion we forgot Jamilah who was asleep. My husband realized that she was still in the house and ran back, but Jamilah was not in her bed! In a panic he turned round and then saw her standing in the other doorway, crying. She had stood up alone for the first time in her life and had toddled out of the room on her own legs!' She continues:

> Tal al Zaatar was a nightmare during the seventeen months of the siege. We were surrounded from the very start, and the Fascists did not allow any food to be transported into the camp. The liberation movement tried to break through their lines on several occasions to create a corridor to rescue us, but they never succeeded, the Fascists were too strong . . . . They wanted to starve us out! We had to break into the food stores and factories that were in the camp, owned by rich Lebanese people. We found chickpeas, lentils and other beans. We pulverized lentils to make bread, but most of the time we lived on thin soups. Cigarettes we made of vine leaves, tea as well! Towards the end we had nothing but lentils left. Throughout the siege the Fascists had one motto: 'Shoot the children first, so that they can't grow up to be soldiers!' For the same reason they shot off the heels of Palestinian children. At the beginning of the Civil War, when it was still possible to move with some freedom in Beirut, the right wing would kidnap young Muslim boys and cut off their fingers to make sure they wouldn't be able to pull the trigger of a machine gun.

While talking, Um Fahdi is becoming more and more agitated. The tears are gone now and she makes wild gestures. The younger children have gone to sleep, but Rim and Fahdi sit behind their schoolbooks listening to their mother.

> In June 1976 the Syrians joined the war on the side of the Fascists to stop the left wing taking power in Lebanon. If they hadn't come in at that moment, we would have been all right! Until that moment the Syrians had remained passive and the Palestinians were able to receive weapons via Syria from the USSR and China. But when the Syrians joined the Fascists, the deliveries were blocked. Our Palestinian commando soldiers had to fight the Syrians too, not only in Tal al Zaatar but in the north around Tripoli, in the

'At night the mothers went out to get water. The wells were in open squares which were under fire the whole time. The mothers kissed their children goodbye before going out of the house, because they didn't know whether they would ever see them again.' This is the story of a child at the Women's Union home for orphans from Tal al Zaatar. Only four out of ten women returned, the rest were killed. The woman with the water bucket (in the middle of the painting) appears in many of the children's drawings, just like tanks, dead people (on the right) and crying houses (on the left).

mountains, on the road to Damascus, in Saida . . . we had too many fronts . . . we couldn't manage it . . . what were our chances?

Many people felt a deep despair and at times I felt like giving up. But we tried to support each other. We must hold out, we said to ourselves, or else we'll die. The most important thing was to support our commando soldiers, to encourage them not to lay down their weapons.

Um Fahdi helped in one of the make-shift clinics which had been set up in a shelter. She looked after thirteen injured people.

But there was no medicine! Only salt and water and the

bandages of those who had died, which we washed and used
again. Most of the injured died within two days, usually of
gangrene, which was the worst problem. It was catching and
spread like wildfire among the injured. We had no pain-
killers . . . but for the injured, the worst thing was knowing
that they were dying . . . . My mother died of gangrene. It
took a week. She was injured by shell splinters when a shell
hit her kitchen. If we had had medicines, she would have
been alive today. Instead she had to die a slow death while
gangrene spread through her body. Until the very end she
kept asking how the siege was going, how far the Fascists
had come and whether they had started negotiating with the
PLO.

Um Fahdi cries silently as she remembers. 'Abu Fahdi buried
my mother in a shallow grave and covered her body with some
corrugated iron and some stones. It was dangerous, they were
firing at him all the time! Then he put a little stick on her grave
so that we could find her when the whole thing was over. One
week later he was killed himself.'

Um Fahdi tells us how they ran out of food and ammunition
during the last days of the siege and how the remaining children
began to die from thirst and malnutrition. In the end no one dared
to leave the shelters. Weeks passed when no one saw the sky.
Thousands of dying, starving people were crammed into the dark
shelters while death reigned in the bombed-out, blown-up alleys
of the camp.

Tal al Zaatar capitulated in August 1976.

'The Fascists promised us safe-conduct out of Tal al Zaatar.
We didn't trust them but we had no choice. The children and I
were among the last to leave the camp. Many had tried to flee
through the mountains . . . .' Um Fahdi falls silent. She remembers
the scenes of the day the camp was evacuated.

We started to walk from the camp. The Fascists were
standing in rows on either side of us. No one said a word,
they just looked at us. At first, there was a ghostly silence.
After a few hundred yards we saw the bodies of those who
had gone before us. They started to pick out our young men
. . . . The Fascists were like mad dogs. . . . one of them lined up
fifteen young men in front of a wall and made us watch
while they were executed. . . I held my hand over Jamilah's

eyes, I was so frightened they'd choose Fahdi ... I was crying all the time. In one place they made me spit on a picture of Yasser Arafat, or else they would have shot me and the children ... I spat and I spat ... and they sneered. The young Fascists dragged our young women off to be raped ....

Tears stream from Um Fahdi's eyes, and she stops to clear her voice.

Just before we reached the square in front of the National Museum in West Beirut, they started to shoot old and injured people ... and at the museum we ran as fast as we could across the square to the Red Cross lorries on the other side, towards safety ... the Fascists still firing after us at random. Those who waited by the lorries could do nothing, they were as helpless as we were ... 1,500 people were killed during the march from Tal al Zaatar to the museum ...

Um Fahdi can no longer speak. The children have put down their textbooks. Fahdi has started to hum a tune and Rim is singing. 'Sing louder,' Um Fahdi shouts between her tears. The children's voices fill the room and reach out into the alley beyond.

Tal al Zaatar *yayouni,*
Tal al Zaatar *yayouni* ...
Tal al Zaatar, my eyes ...
Tal al Zaatar, my eyes ...
The world will do homage to me
because of your resistance,
at night, oh Zaatar, at night!
We are Palestinians, we are Palestinians ...
Death does not frighten us,
at night, oh Zaatar, at night!

The children's singing fades away and we are left sitting silently around the hot plate. Um Fahdi leans forward, concentrating hard. What she wants to say is very important to her. She changes, her eyes are dry and her hoarse voice steadies. 'Before Tal al Zaatar weapons used to frighten me,' she says. 'I dared not even touch the butt of a gun .... Before Tal al Zaatar I was not political, I was remote, removed from my people's problem. But Tal al Zaatar changed everything! Today the liberation struggle is

the most important thing in my life. I wanted to become a
commando soldier. But I'm a woman, I have children to look
after. It's not possible. If I were younger and unmarried, then
. . . but I cook for our champions of liberation and that, too, is
a way of supporting the Revolution.'

It has grown late and we have to leave, Um Fahdi comes out
with us into the alley. It's very dark and we can only sense the
crescent moon behind the clouds. 'You know,' Um Fahdi says,
looking up, 'now I love Tal al Zaatar more than ever . . . because
my husband and my parents, my whole family are buried there.
I'd like to go back to see their graves.' But Um Fahdi knows that
she can't go back. If she were discovered there, she would be shot.
Probably she doesn't even know what the thyme-covered hill
where Tal al Zaatar once stood, now looks like.

Tal al Zaatar simply does not exist any more. When we visited
the place, we saw an immense pile of rubble on the slope down
towards Beirut. As soon as the camp had been evacuated, the
Fascists devastated the area, going over it with bulldozers, level-
ling the houses to the ground, deleting every trace of the 30,000
people who had once lived there.

13. Nimri and Mohammed Get Married

The gates of heaven have been open for days and the rain has made great puddles in the uneven alleys and filled the shell holes with water. But on this Sunday the Mediterranean wind is blowing and drying the mud to sand, helped by the sun. The flies, sheltering from the wind, stubbornly settle on anything edible.

As usual, a group of people — older women, soldiers and children — are standing outside Abu Nimmer's shop but, since it's Sunday, there are men there as well, gathering to find out what's happening. Abu Nimmer, a stout little man with white close-cropped hair and a tidy moustache, spends every day standing in his small, dark shop. The wooden shelves are sagging in the middle from the weight of dusty tins, 'Donated by the People of the United States of America — Not to be Sold or Exchanged' it says, on a sack of flour in one corner.

Mohammed, a twenty-one-year-old guerrilla, comes into the shop with a couple of other guerrillas to buy cigarettes. He looks somewhat untidy. A lock of wet hair falls onto his forehead and his expression is stiff, even stern. He tries to smile but can't. 'My wedding party is today . . . I hope you can come?' he stutters.

Abu Nimmer nods and the soldiers grin. This wedding has been a topic of conversation in this part of the camp for some time. But, having waited three years, the day has finally come when Mohammed is to collect his seventeen-year-old bride, Nimri, and the idea terrifies him.

Mohammed and Nimri fell in love when he was her weapons instructor in *Zahrat*, the Fatah youth organization for girls between the ages of eight and fifteen. Nimri was only fourteen, but even then he decided to marry her. Mohammed has visited Nimri's home often and regularly, because he is a fellow soldier and workmate of her older brother, Ibrahim. But he didn't propose until this year when he went to Ibrahim to express his wish. Ibrahim, since his father's death, makes all family decisions. He requested two weeks to think about it. He then asked his uncles whether any of them had expected Nimri to marry one of their sons. He also asked Nimri, as, according to Islam, a girl cannot be married to someone against her will. Nimri said, 'Yes', there was nothing she wanted more. So, in this case there were no problems.

However, according to Islamic tradition, a girl consents with silence. Thus the pressure on a girl from a traditional family can be so hard that there is practically no chance of her going against its will. Traditionally, the honour and status of the family are put above all else in the Palestinian community, and whom the daughter marries is an important family consideration. In the old days it was even more so. The daughters' marriages created economic and political alliances for the heads of families, and this affected the family's social standing in the village. Many parents still prefer it if the girl marries within the family, usually by marrying her first cousin.

But much has changed for the Palestinian refugees. Families have been dispersed, there is general poverty in the camps and no one has land to protect or extend by marriage. Moreover, the Liberation movement has taken over the traditionally powerful roles which some of the families held in Palestine. Family alliances are no longer so important and the basis of the old marriage tradition has been weakened. More consideration now is given to the emotions. We hear more about girls who choose their own husbands. It is becoming increasingly common that the father only asks his daughter that her future husband should ask for his agreement as a matter of form, a pure ritual.

Mohammed and Nimri have been engaged for seven weeks. According to Islamic custom, Mohammed has to pay a bride price for Nimri. But Mohammed is an orphan and also on a low wage as a guerrilla. Guerrillas are popular with girls, but this honour provides no money and Mohammed can't pay the bride price. Instead he and Ibrahim have arranged a 'nominal bridal transaction' — Mohammed pays a symbolic sum at the wedding instead of the enormous sum quoted in the contract. In the Palestinian exile community this has become the rule rather than the exception. No one can afford the tradition.

Nimri is pleased, she is wholly against being sold as merchandise. More and more girls feel this way. However, another aspect of the transaction does remain — the sum Mohammed

will have to pay if he divorces her. In this case he would have to
pay Nimri and her family £1,500, a sum that would be almost
impossible to raise for most camp Palestinians.

Once the marriage contract has been written with the *mufti,*
the Muslim priest, the couple are legally married although they
will not live together until the wedding celebration is over. War
and bombing may even separate a couple and prevent them from
ever celebrating the wedding and living together. If a woman bears
a child in the period between the signature of the contract and the
wedding, the child is considered legitimate, provided that the
husband recognizes the child.

It is a fairly peaceful day for a wedding party and, on this
particular Sunday, four different weddings are being celebrated
in Rashidiyeh. At Nimri's home preparations are well underway. A
relation from Beirut has brought her a cassette of John Travolta's
'Grease' and this is played incessantly, annoying the others. They
want to hear Um Kaltoum, the much-loved Egyptian singer who
caused more Egyptians to leave their homes to attend her funeral
than the great Arab nationalist leader, Nasser himself, when he
died. From the room where Nimri is seated, the scent of powder
and eau-de-cologne mingle with the smell of cardamon and
freshly made coffee from the kitchen. Nimri sits stiffly on the sofa
while around her her sisters and female relations hover, chatter
and help to arrange her hair. On the wall above, magazine pictures
of Arab singers are placed next to those of the Osmond brothers,
and beside these is a Palestinian map embroidered in cross-stitch
with a crocheted Palestinian flag. Her sisters are normally busy
doing embroidery, crocheting or sewing on commission — the
traditional ways in which women make some money. But now
they are busy with Nimri's make-up: thick green eye shadow, mas-
cara and dark red lipstick.

Nimri herself is not 'all there', she sits motionless and her gaze
is distant. She, like Mohammed, has waited a long time for this
day to arrive. Within a few hours she will be a married woman
with all that that entails. She will leave her parents' and sisters'
house and go to live with Mohammed, running her own household which is a role she has been trained for since she was a little
girl. Then her oldest brother will no longer make decisions for
her, instead they will be made by Mohammed. But she will have
more freedom as a married woman — freedom to speak to whom
she chooses, and to decide what she wants to do. At the end of
the evening, once all the guests have left, Mohammed and Nimri

will shut the door of their house, and they will be alone together
for the first time. Tonight Nimri will lose her virginity.

An unmarried woman watches over her unbroken hymen, and
it's easy to remain a virgin in a community with the strict social
control of Rashidiyeh. Nimri has been guarded and she couldn't
have even talked to a boy in the street without other people
knowing about it. They would immediately have suspected a love
affair, the gossip would have increased and Nimri's reputation
would have been endangered. That would be all that was needed.
If a girl has lost her virginity before the wedding night, her
husband can decide to keep quiet about it, or choose to throw
her out, thus breaking the marriage contract. The girl would have
to return to her family. The men of her family would then have to
decide what to do about her. They might let her stay at home, but
the girl would be disgraced for life and never again respected. The
honour of the family would have been ruined, a thing so terrible
that the family may even choose to kill her. However, this is
becoming very unusual nowadays. Older, more traditional
Palestinian men and women feel that this is what has to be done.
But the younger ones are ashamed of this custom which they say
is disgraceful.

At two o'clock Nimri's wedding party is in full swing. There are
almost only women present. Mohammed is holding a party for his
male friends in another courtyard. In the narrow alley outside
Nimri's house, children and adults are crowded together. Girls
are standing in clusters in the courtyard and the beat of the tablas
is heard in the room where Nimri sits. More and more women
drop in, the women from our street, Um Abdullah, Um Ali and
her daughters, Um Immad and Mouna and her sisters, and Mouna's
friend Shahirah.

Shahirah works as a children's nurse at the Red Crescent clinic
in Rashidiyeh and is known as the best dancer in the camp. And
now she dances, rolling her hips and wriggling her arms in an Arab
dance to the rhythm of the drum, sending dark, challenging looks
through her dense eyelashes, bending her agile body backwards,
so far that her black hair trails on the floor, throwing her body
up, her upper body vibrating, shaking and flowing into new
movements.

The women and little girls take turns to dance alone or in pairs
in the more and more crowded space in front of the bride. The

room is soon a surging ocean of black heads mingling with white
headscarfs bobbing up and down. The women clap their hands,
urging each other to dance. Spirits rise higher and higher, and
some women sing in loud, shrill, throaty tones. Different women
lead the singing. Old traditional songs are mixed with new revolutionary battle songs:

> I'm a *fedayi,** my sister's a *fedaya*
> My brother's a *fedayi*!
> The whole Arab people are *fedayeen*!
> Fighting Zionism!
>
> The good water of the well is only for *fedayeen*!
> They will be victorious over Zionists and Carter!

In another room Ibrahim and the men are drinking tea. No alcohol
is served. The women cheer and shout when he enters the women's
room to dance.

> Ya Ibrahim, you're like a jasmine!
> Your family is large!
> You're tall and handsome!
> Your aunts are singing for you!
> Yi yi yi yi yi . . .
> We'll offer you something
> worth more than gold!
> Yi yi yi yi!

The sun is filtering through a shell hole in the ceiling and
Nimri sits serious and dignified in the middle of the ecstasy,
behaving in the manner expected of a bride and plucking
nervously at a paper handkerchief on her lap.

People come and go, wandering from one wedding to another.
The tablas from Mohammed's wedding party can be heard in the
neighbouring courtyard. Because Mohammed is an orphan, he
has been received as a son in the home of the dancer Shahirah and
is now being celebrated there. Under the vines in the courtyard
the men are sitting in a circle, older men and boys wearing the
guerrilla uniform. The fact that Mohammed is a guerrilla gives
the celebration a slightly different atmosphere. Several friends

*Fedayi is the Arabic word for guerilla or freedom fighters;
fedayi is masculine, *fedaya* feminine, *fedayeen* plural.

of his have come home from the front to join in. The men's circle is broken by the occasional woman. Mohammed himself sits serious and sleek-haired, in civilian clothes amongst all the uniforms.

The revolutionary mood has considerably affected the wedding tradition and the men are almost exclusively singing battle songs, dancing with their machine guns — *Kalashnikovs* — raised over their heads. They sing the song in honour of the *Kalashnikov.*

Kalashnikov, Kalashnikov,
Let your bullet fly!
We've returned with the RPG*
Done a Klasch operation
and come back again!
Ya hala! Ya hala!
Ras al Nakoura will meet us!

A guerrilla plays a small metal flute — the *shebaba.* Another plays the accordion. The beat of the tablas urges one man after another to join the dance inside the circle. No one is allowed to remain seated, they must all dance in honour of Mohammed.

* Bazooka, a light anti-tank weapon.

'*Yalla*, Abu Nimmer!' — Dance! Dance! . . . the men call to the
grocer, who eventually lets himself be persuaded. He takes a
machine gun in one hand, takes some hesitant steps following the
beat of the drum, but soon lets himself go in a quicker rhythm.
The men roar and cheer, clapping their hands. Abu Nimmer smiles
under his moustache and beads of perspiration appear on his forehead. Shahirah comes on to the floor and dances with him, the
men bellow even louder and in the end she is alone on the floor.
The men start singing.

> I have broken the chains,
> the symbol of my degradation!
> I have crushed the man who flogged me
> and caused my tragedy!
>
> I have come out of my prison!
> We are the sons of Fatah . . .
> Fatah created the People's Revolution
> and its fedayi army
> paving the way for our return!

Suddenly the whole party gets up and leaves the courtyard,
singing. Mohammed is going to collect Nimri. As he walks into
Nimri's courtyard, everyone steps aside, leaving a narrow corri-
dor for the bride.

It all happens very quickly, they are holding an olive branch
together. People are crowding in from all directions, children
disappear amongst trampling feet, they all want to leave the
courtyard at the same time to walk close to Mohammed and
Nimri, and the alley doesn't have room for them all. Children fall
and cry, adults shout and run after the bride and groom who are
leading the procession towards Mohammed's house, their hands
raised around the olive branch. The bride and groom are set down
on two chairs in front of their house, one flower arrangement after
another is placed at their feet, people sing and clap hands and
crowd together on top of the wall to catch a glimpse of the
spectacle. Family and friends go up one by one, saying: '*Mabrouk!*'
— Congratulations! The dancing starts again, the bride and groom
are forced onto the floor, they dance together, suddenly awkward.
The tablas will sound for many hours before Mohammed and
Nimri can finally close the door of their home.

Later that week we go and see Mohammed and Nimri, together

with Shahirah and her mother, who want to give them a gift of
beautifully wrapped tea glasses and some drinking glasses. It is
customary to visit the couple during the week following their
wedding to congratulate them and present a gift. Mohammed and
Nimri don't go out at all during the course of the week but remain
in to receive their visitors. *'Mabrouk!'* Shahirah says, handing them
her gift. Mohammed seems incredibly happy and holds Nimri
close. The parcel is left unopened. The house has already changed
its character and the beds are meticulously arranged with
crocheted pillow-covers. There are flower arrangements everywhere. Both of them are dressed up, in high spirits and they can't
hide their love for each other. At the end of the week Mohammed
will return to his work and Nimri will remain at home to look
after the house.

14. My Little Brother Decides

After visiting Mohammed and Nimri we return to Shahirah's house for a meal. A little later Mohammed comes over and asks for some bread. Although he is so much in love, he complains about having to stay in and not being able to see his friends for a week. When he has left the room, the humorous, smiling, strong Shahirah frowns. '*He* is bored after four days! What about the women who have to stay at home all their lives! Just because the men have said so!' She grows angrier and angrier.

> It seems to me that a woman was not born to manage her own life. Look at me! My father is old and sick, and therefore my little brother makes decisions for me, my little brother whom I looked after when he was a baby! He is six years younger, but he is the eldest son. He thinks he knows everything! Of course, he goes out much more than I do, he meets other people, but he decides who *my* friends should be. He wants me to quit smoking, girls shouldn't be smoking, he says, and it costs money. O'kay, okay, I say and go on smoking!

Shahirah furiously flings her head back.

> He himself smokes! But I often object to him, I refuse to do as he tells me. That makes him really angry, he shouts and screams like a small child. But isn't it strange? At the same time I admire him and his strength. When we quarrel at home I sometimes think it's like listening to music. We've got that kind of music most of the time. When I lived in Beirut training to be a children's nurse, the fighting and firing also sounded like music in the end. We fight our battles at the

front, against the enemy, against imperialism, but we also
fight our battles in the home. Nimri and Mohammed will
fight many wars in their home.

Shahirah believes that there are many things which young
Palestinian women want to change. But their families prevent
them — not only the men, but also the older women. She points
to a picture on the wall, a young woman with a machine gun slung
across her shoulder against a red background.

Dalal! I shall try to be even stronger! Like Dalal who broke
with tradition and went to the front, living with the men. I
met her several times. Now she is a heroine. No one would
dream of criticizing her. But I am strong too, I also am a
guerrilla soldier — *fedaya* — though in my own way! I work
for the Revolution here in the clinic and I support my
family.

Shahirah earns 378 lirah a month (about £57) and keeps 15 lirah
for her own personal use. Her younger brother, who is a member
of the camp militia, has a salary of 400 lirah a month (about £60)
but gives the family only 100 lirah. 'But he studies as well in Sour,
and that costs him 100 lirah, plus books and food and group taxi
fares. And I suppose he goes to the cinema and to restaurants and
. . . well, you know what men are like . . . ' she says resignedly.

Shahirah gives the impression of being rather a proud, tough,
young woman, a woman who knows her own mind and one who
is prepared to fight for the things she believes in. A strong woman
within her traditional role, but one who does not quite dare go all
the way. This is often the case here — the girls give way to
family pressure.

She looks up, slowly twisting a lock of hair between her fingers.

When I'm on my own I usually think of the plans I have for
my own family, how I'd like to bring up my children. I want
to teach my children to discuss issues, to study and learn all
about new things. I want to support them, not oppose them.
They should be courageous, both boys and girls. They will
liberate Palestine and build a beautiful country where all
people are equal and happy. They must make friends with
the Israelis who stay and try to forgive them what they did
to us. That is my dream!

15. The Heroine

On the wall in Mouna's room is a poster of Dalal Moghrabi, the same poster as the one Shahirah has on her wall. Her picture can be seen everywhere — in homes, in guerrilla offices, in schools and on the windshields of the commando jeeps. It is probably the face most well known to the camp population, after that of Yasser Arafat. She was completely unknown until 11 March 1978 when a blurred picture of a dead woman who had been badly shot was flashed around the world. In Western news agencies, teleprinters rattled out the headline 'A group of Palestinian terrorists have carried out an act of mindless aggression'. The woman in the picture was Dalal, twenty-one, a Palestinian woman from Lebanon and the leader of the 'terrorist group'.

In the West everyone quickly condemned the 'terrorist action' and condolences went streaming in to the Israeli Government. But in the Palestinian camps, people were ecstatic because a group of Palestinians, champions of liberation, had hit Tel Aviv itself, the heart of the enemy and the largest Zionist city.

'Whenever our commandos infiltrate Israel with machine guns and hand grenades, the West roars in abhorrence. But when the Israelis attack our camps with aeroplanes, tanks, gunboats and artillery . . . when thousands of Palestinians are forced to flee and hundreds of them are killed by shells and bursting bombs . . . then they call it retaliation. But why isn't that terrorism? We knew that Israel was planning to invade Southern Lebanon,' she continues. 'They wanted to destroy us, once and for all! Or, as the Israeli leader Mr Begin put it, they wanted to "cut off the arm of the devil". The aim of the Tel Aviv action was to provoke the Israelis into action before they had completed their preparations.' They succeeded. Three days later the Israelis invaded.

This action was also an important milestone for Palestinian

One of the many pictures of Dalal in her parents' home.

women because for the first time in the history of the liberation struggle, a woman had led a guerrilla action inside the
occupied home country! But, more than that, the other twelve
members of her group were men! 'I want to be like Dalal,' young
women will often say with admiration in their voices. 'Dalal was
fine,' men say approvingly. 'She was as good as a man.' Today
Dalal Moghrabi is canonized by the Palestinians. She has become a
martyr, a legend, an idol! As Mouna explains:

> Dalal meant a great deal to us. Before Dalal many people
> laughed at the idea of having female commandos. They
> thought that women were no good at fighting, and when we
> tried to get together a women's brigade a few years ago, we
> were ridiculed by the men. When we asked for weapons, they
> said 'No' and the whole project petered out. Of course we
> have female commandos and of course we have training
> camps for women. But when their training is completed, they
> are sent home again. Because of all this our women don't
> trust themselves when it comes to military action. Their
> confidence has been eroded and they believe that the men are
> better at everything, they've always been told so. Dalal
> showed us that women can do just as well!

But who was Dalal? What made her succeed at things other
Palestinian women only dream of doing? The story of Dalal Moghrabi is the story of a woman who had to fight for the right to
die for her country.

We visited Dalal's mother at her home in the Sabra camp in
South Beirut. The staircase walls were covered with posters of
Dalal and the other members of the Tel Aviv action group. We
knocked on a light blue door and Dalal's mother, a stout woman
dressed in black, opened it. She showed us into a room where the
walls were covered with more pictures of Dalal. While our interpreter explained who we were, Dalal's grandmother joined us. She,
too, was dressed in black and watched us with large, mournful
eyes, and smoked almost continuously throughout the conversation.

'Dalal was very independent,' her mother said. 'She did exactly
what she wanted to do. "I've got self-confidence!" she would
often say. We discovered that she played truant, so, one day, we
followed her and found out that she worked as a nurse for the
commandos. We tried to persuade her to take up her studies
again but she refused. "I must work for my people," she said.

"I must contribute to the Revolution! It's the duty of all
Palestinians!'"

Her eyes widen as she talks. Dalal's mother is Lebanese. Her
father is Palestinian and has always talked to his children about
Palestine. But her mother has always worried about what might
happen if her children were to join the struggle for liberation.
'Dalal joined Fatah and became a telegraph operator. When the
Syrians arrived in Lebanon in 1976, she fought them in the mountains. In 1977 she went to a military training course and, three
months later, passed her exam as a lieutenant.' Dalal's mother
proudly pointed to a certificate, framed in black, on the wall
behind us. It was signed by Yasser Arafat. 'That was when she
started to live in the guerrilla bases in Southern Lebanon. I told
her she was a disgrace to the family. A girl alone amongst so many
boys! People talk! "Don't worry," she said. "My friends respect
me."'

But Dalal had to fight hard to acquire the respect of her male
friends. Mouna's friend Khaled can testify to that. He was on the
same training course as Dalal and they were at the same guerrilla
base. 'Dalal *demanded* of our leaders that she should join the
guerrilla movement. They couldn't reject a person prepared to
join. But it wasn't easy for her. I remember how some of the men
at the base used to talk behind her back. "Oh well," one of them
once said, "In seven months she'll have a big belly." "Why?" I asked
him. "Who would make her pregnant?" I explained that none of
us were there to play around. We were there to fight, and so was
Dalal! Beirut's the place for playing around. The others laughed
and said that her parents would probably come and collect her.'
In fact, Dalal's mother tried to do this.

Dalal's mother continued the story. 'But when I realized that
Dalal slept in her own room with a guard outside, when I saw how
she related to the boys, I stopped worrying . . . . Do you know how
I found out that Dalal was dead? My oldest daughter Rashidah
came in with a newspaper in her hand. "Look at the picture,"
she said. "Yes", I replied, "A girl has become a martyr in
Palestine.' "Don't you recognize the girl?" Rashidah asked.
"Don't you see that it's our Dalal?" I couldn't believe it! I just
stared at the picture! But when I did realize that the girl in the
picture was my daughter, I beat my chest and cried. And when I
went out in my mourning clothes, the neighbours came and told
me to wear brighter clothing. "Be happy!" they said. "Don't cry!
No one has carried out such an operation since Palestine was first

occupied. The Koran tells us that all martyrs go to heaven.'"

Dalal's grandmother began to cry, her body trembling with emotion. 'Dalal was so wonderful, I loved her . . . . She liked my cooking so much! The last time she came here to visit us, she gave me a particularly affectionate kiss when she said goodbye . . . but then I didn't know what was to happen . . . . '

We also met Assad, a guerrilla and an original member of Dalal's group. This group had made a couple of attempts to enter Israel from Lebanon by sea but their previous attempts had been interrupted by bad weather. The reason why Assad is still alive and active within the liberation movement is because he fell ill and had to stay behind while the others made their final, successful attempt.

'Dalal was a patriot,' he told us. 'She was very politically aware! She understood the relationship between Palestine and the world, and what she did was part of the world struggle.' Assad considered Dalal a strong support during preparations for the operation. She made sure no one was left alone, as it is then that people lose confidence and grow anxious.

> This was necessary if the operation was to succeed. We were trained hard and we constantly encouraged each other so that finally, we knew exactly where each one of us stood. We became as one person. We looked to the future and that meant a lot to the strength of the group. We all knew what was before us. Death! Many foreigners believe that we like to die, to commit suicide. That is wrong! Death must have a meaning! Our death was to be the way to real life, a better life in Palestine. We did it for the people, for the children, for the country. For the future! There is nothing more beautiful a person can do than die for his home country!

> The night before we left, Dalal suggested that we write something on the notice board. Together we wrote in our blood: 'Palestine, we're coming.' The last thing Dalal wrote before going down to the waiting boat was: 'I, Dalal, am prepared to die for my country. Do not cry, my mother.'

Dalal is an example for this girl from the Pioneers, the PFLP youth organization.

16. 'One's Ears Become Like Radar'

The cigarette smoke lies like a fog in the low tent, and in the dim light of an oil lamp, ten guerrillas sit close together. They are holding their machine guns between their knees and are wearing heavy boots: they are prepared. Outside the tent, in the dark under the olive trees, the guards talk quietly together.

We had been spending a few days at a Palestinian guerrilla base in Arkoub in the mountains of South-east Lebanon. The date was 19 December 1978, and Lebanon has begun to erupt again after a long period of relative calm. In Beirut fighting between the Syrians and the Lebanese right wing has again broken out, and in Southern Lebanon artillery duels have started between Palestinians on the one hand, and Israelis and the Lebanese right wing under Major Saad Haddad, on the other.

Throughout the day we had heard the thunder of the bombardment against the Palestinian stronghold of Nabatiya, in the mountains some ten kilometres away.

Then suddenly the walkie-talkie crackled, the conversation in the tent stopped and everybody listened, their eyes focused on the transmitter. A very long message announced that the Israelis had bombed the Sour area and the Bourj al Shemaleh camp during the day. Palestinians had carried out an action in Israel and injured several Israelis. So, the bombing of the camps had begun again. We immediately thought of the people in the camps around Sour.

During the night there was a great deal of movement in the tent. The men slept in shifts and at daybreak all the guerrillas were tense, but in high spirits, as they waited for something to happen. As the sun rose over a ridge on Mount Hermon, an almost inaudible, swift metallic sound could be heard whistling through the air. A watchful, experienced ear reacts very quickly. The

Palestinian guerrillas in the mountains of Southern Lebanon. They are looking towards their home country, the mountains in the distance. None of them have ever been there.

explosion was somewhere nearby and the roar resounded in the valley; an echo reproducing
·mountainsides for ten to fifteen seconds, before the bird song could be heard again.

In an instant everyone was down in the trenches surrounding the tents between the olive trees. Several bombs hit the adjacent ground in quick succession. 'Haddad! They are trying to pin-point us from Marjeyoun,' a guerrilla hissed. Haddad's shells fell over the area for three hours that morning. The Palestinian artillery returned the fire from its batteries further north. 'It's a good. thing they are firing, as we can then guess their positions. It means we'll know when we have to return fire from the bases,' the lieutenant of our base remarked. Haddad's shells never found our base and neither did they find the others. Not a Lebanese village was hit either, although a farmer was killed in an olive grove.

The violence continued and gradually escalated. Artillery duels continue unremittingly in Southern Lebanon between the Palestinian side and the Israelis who have liaised with Major Haddad's right-wing Lebanese forces. A new guerrilla operation promoted an Israeli infantry advance into Lebanon and an attack on a Palestinian stronghold north of the eastern branch of the Litani River On the following day the Israelis landed troops one kilometre south of Rashidiyeh in a little village called Ras al Ain. They stormed a deserted house but were forced to flee in a helicopter when the Palestinian guerrillas opened fire with machine guns. During the second week of January 1979, the Israelis fired at the camps of Rashidiyeh and Bourj al Shemaleh for several nights running, and tension was further increased when the Palestinians responded by firing rockets at some villages in Northern Israel. The Palestinian guerrillas then carried out an operation in Metullah, a village in Northern Israel, and one man was killed. Everyone awaited Israel's next move.

Then, on 21 January 1979, Abu Hassan, the PLO security chief, was blown up in a car in Verdun Street in Beirut, together with his four bodyguards. Six years earlier, the Zionists had shot dead three eminent PLO men in a flat in the same street. Abu Hassan's death was on the radio and in everyone's mouth: 'Another Zionist terror action.' In Damascus the PLO National Council were meeting. Yasser Arafat left immediately to go to Beirut.

On the same evening we drove down to Rashidiyeh The road along the coast was dark and shiny from the rain. Palestinian military jeeps and lorries carrying bananas and oranges were the only vehicles we saw on the way. As we approached the south, we occasionally glimpsed the backs of Palestinian guerrillas carrying machine guns and bazookas across their shoulders. Rashidiyeh was asleep when we arrived.

We had been away from the camp for five weeks. We had left it as the nights grew cooler, and the few deciduous trees began to shed their leaves and the prayer calls were heard five times a day. We remember a living Rashidiyeh . . . with alleys full of playing children, groups of chattering, laughing, working women squatting outside the gateways; the lumbering old men; the schoolchildren in their beige school jackets; the spontaneous celebrations alive with the steady beat of the tablas; the dancing

and singing . . . and the war which constantly reverberated with
thousands of voices and Arab music. But this time we find naked
vines standing out against the sky, black and wet. The grass has
grown several feet with all the rain, and the rooms are cold and
raw, the floors icy-cold. The night was star-lit. Bomb-lit! Israeli
bombers prefer to see their target, they abhor bad weather with
cloud and rain . . . .

A grey rainy dawn was breaking as we awoke the next day to
a distant threatening thunder and Um Ali's shrill call out in the
alley. *'Yalla!'* — Hurry up! 'Down into the shelters!' Quick steps
trampled the gravel, several voices called out, a door was slammed
shut but the noise was drowned by a new, powerful roar. Um Ali
laughed. 'Go back to bed! It was nothing! Only thunder!'

How many people in Rashidiyeh were awakened by the same
noise? Was it an omen . . ? The Israelis had been dropping shells
over the camps for several nights in succession and Israeli planes
had been running constant low reconnaissance flights. Many
people slept in the shelters. Anxiety and tension had spread.
People slept badly and were startled by every sound. Such
constant watch, and tense nerves can make people over-sensitive
to noise. Any little sound can be interpreted as an approaching
raid or as bombs hitting the ground. There is no relief.

That morning the minaret stood in silent watch over the alleys
of the camp. Allah did not call people to prayer over the loudspeaker. Still, the cocks crowed and the camp came to life. The air
was filled with sounds, albeit deadened by the steady, heavy rain.
It was bitingly cold and damp. A group of women stood bent over
the water-conduit, washing up. They had bare feet and their damp
clothes clung to their bodies. The children in our alley danced the
twist when it stopped raining, they were not going to school. The
men could be seen outside: Abu Ali and Abu Immad, who were
usually away during the day, stood around, idle and restless
amongst the houses, carrying their machine guns.

The door of Um Immad's house was closed. Mouna gently
opened it and greeted us. In the middle of the room the children
were crowded about the oil heater. The warmth did not reach the
old lady who was sitting wrapped up in a thick winter coat with
blankets around her legs. Um Immad's eyes were vague and dark.
Her body was heavy, the baby was due at any moment. Mouna
sank down on the floor next to her youngest sister, tucked her
legs beneath her and gently massaged her temples.

I'm tired, very tired. We're all tired . . . it's been going on for
a month . . . our ears have become like radar. Last week was
dreadful, two women were killed by Israeli shells in Bourj
al Shemaleh, 70 houses were damaged and 15 totally destroyed. In Rashidiyeh we have shelters enough, we've always
been most exposed, but in Bourj al Shemaleh there are not
shelters for everyone. I've been awake all night and have
visited their shelters, I have visited the injured in the
hospitals, have gone round talking to the men and women
from the houses that were destroyed . . . I've tried to
convince them to stay . . . but it's very, very difficult. They
want to go north to Saida and Beirut. They don't want to
die! Thirty per cent of the population in Bourj al Shemaleh
have left their homes.

Mouna leant her head on her hands. 'That's exactly what the
Israelis want! They bomb the camps to make us flee, they tire us
out, they play with our brains . . . trying to break our morale.
I'm very concerned as to how we can make people hold out, to
keep resisting . . . .'
A couple of young women have come in, unnoticed; they sat
down next to Mouna, talking quietly with each other. The
children talk about Abu Hassan's death and look at the pictures
in the newspapers we have brought them. 'Everything is shut
now,' Mouna said, turning to us. 'Everything except the clinics and
hospitals. Only a fifth of the children go to school . . . the day
nurseries are closed, the parents are afraid of sending the children
there . . . but we shall try to convince them otherwise so that we
can open them again tomorrow. We've certainly got new things
to do now in the Women's Union! Mouna gave a hoarse
little laugh and hummed along to the song the children were
singing.
Kaboom!
It was over in a flash. The strong, sharp explosion which made
the ground tremble, the house shiver. The plastic sheets in the
windows were sucked in and then torn off their nails by the strong
shock-wave. Our heads pounded, then there was a sudden sound
of shattering glass and people screaming. Everything happened
at breakneck speed. Everyone ran to the door and out. The
children ran as fast as they possibly could towards the shelter,
terrified hens crackled and fluttered in all directions. The effect
of the explosion could still be felt minutes afterwards. A large

white cloud of smoke rose up a few streets away.

Kaboom! Kaboom!

Several hits. Further away.

'From the sea,' somebody shouted. There was a sudden crush on on the steps down to the shelter. Children fell over. Soldiers in uniform with machine guns watched the entrance. Mouna led her grandmother down the steps, helping hands reached out towards her. The shelter was already full of women and children.

Kaboom! Kaboom!

The earth trembled heavily with the shocks and the walls of the shelter vibrated. People were quiet, very quiet, even the youngest were too frightened to make a noise. A nearby car revved up. Soft sunlight filtered past all the bodies on the crowded staircase. Women and children sat huddled together on the floor of the small shelter.

Mouna had disappeared. Um Immad sat with her eyes closed and her lips moving, holding her belly. Pain marked her face at each explosion. Her youngest child was sobbing, holding her hands over her ears and pressing herself against her mother. The old lady mumbled quietly to herself about Allah's greatness. The air was stale and anxious. Rashidiyeh was being hit several times a minute, those endless minutes which never seem to end. Um Ali sat with her eyes closed and appeared to be unaffected by the terror around her. *'Tayran!'* — Aeroplanes! somebody shouted. There was a hush throughout the room, the message spread like wildfire, as the word was repeated. Air bombing means fragmentation bombs, perhaps napalm, a sticky, burning paste which can slowly trickle down the shelter steps, and, on touching the skin, burns into the muscles. It is impossible to remove it. The children cried out in terror. 'Shut up! It's not aeroplanes!' a man from the door of the shelters shouted.

Towards the end of the attack which lasted forty-five minutes the shells fell at increasing intervals. Then it was quiet. The people in the shelter laughed loudly with relief.

Heated voices were heard in the alley. What had happened? Who had died? Which houses had been hit? Mouna came running along, darting between the houses, her body slightly bent, her arms hugging her chest. Behind her ran children in school coats; they had spent the duration of the raid in the school shelter and now they threw themselves into the arms of their mothers. Um Ali burst into tears, one of her children was missing! Mouna talked quickly, everybody listened soundlessly. The old camp has taken

most of the shells, no one has been killed but an old man lay
dying. Many houses had been damaged . . . . Group taxis were
taking the injured to the hospital in Sour.

One hundred 155mm shells had fallen over Rashidiyeh, fired
from Israel seventeen kilometres to the south. Half an hour later
shells began to explode again among the houses in Bourj al
Shemaleh three kilometres away. Everyone returned to the
shelters and for an hour we sat listening to the distant explosions. The sunlight was blinding when we came up again. The
laundry on the roofs was flapping in the wind. Broken power
lines lay fallen severed by bomb splinters. One soldier had been
hit by splinter and blood dripped from his hand. Wherever we
looked we saw pieces of scattered splinter, metal fragments,
large and small, spiked and sharp as knives, that can cut into
soft skin and cause deep stomach wounds: metal fragments had
even bored through concrete walls, and spread a long way from
the place where they first hit the ground.

Shortly after the last shell had fallen, the exodus began. Older
men, young women and children begged for seats in the taxis
which were already full to overflowing. The price of a journey
to Sour had doubled ten times, twenty times, a trip to Saida
could cost 80 lirah instead of the normal three. People packed
themselves into the cars, each on top of the other, they hung out
of the unclosed doors as the cars scraped the ground with their
heavy loads of people. Those who could not get in started to walk
instead. Everyone travelled north, towards security, to relations if
they had them, or into uncertainty if they did not. They leave all
they have behind, but at least they leave with their lives intact.
The exodus went on all afternoon. One house after another was
locked up, and one car after another was loaded with people,
suitcases and mattresses. The main street which was usually
peaceful and almost rurally quiet became an inferno of hooting
queuing cars.

Um Immad's family were collected by a relative from Saida
that afternoon. On the small platform of the lorry they were
packed in together with a couple of other families from our
street. There was no room for luggage. We did not even have
time to say goodbye. The children waved and made the sign of
victory as the lorry disappeared around the street corner.

But Mouna stayed together with Abu Immad. Those who left

were women and children, the men remained to defend the camp in case of attack. It was horrifying to see all these people leaving Rashidiyeh. Life in the alleys had ended. The remaining children had stopped playing, they stood silently next to the adults, looking at the ruins of houses that had been hit. Men and women stood together in large groups, talking quietly about the damage. No one raised their voices, no one laughed and no one even gesticulated.

The atmosphere was stern and serious, but beneath the calm lay hatred. Most women and nearly all the men carried machine guns. We went from one house to another with the Chairman of the People's Committee, Abu Ahmed. He took notes of the damage wrought — the houses that had been hit and the numbers of people injured. A group of ten to twenty people followed us everywhere, new faces joined us, others stopped to talk to friends and relatives who had had their houses destroyed. We saw remnants of homes which had been, only that morning, inhabited and lively. A piece of a flowery mattress protrudes from under a collapsed wall . . . a roof has fallen in and knocked down the walls of the alley, barricading it . . . a kitchen without a roof, and tumbled walls, fallen shelves, and shattered jars of olives, rice, lentils mingled with the concrete on the floor . . . living-rooms have furniture turned upside down, broken plates and coffee-cups, the shards of mirrors, of memories . . . A thin mist of sand and cement hangs over the camp. The UNRWA office has been hit, paper and shattered glass have been flung everywhere . . . a UNRWA car peppered by hundreds of exploding fragments, its tyres flat while oil bleeds from the engine . . . . In many places we saw women sitting on the floors of their kitchens, making bread, baking with the only flour they have, to take on the journey.

We felt very uncomfortable about producing our cameras and taking photographs. But women and men who have recovered from the shock came to fetch us, they pulled us along to the remains of their ruined homes, pointing: 'Look at this! Look at my house! Ruins! Take pictures and show the people in your home country what the Zionists do against us!' Everywhere we watched women sweeping the broken glass and cement from the floors, piling mattresses, cleaning . . . . The old people just stood watching. They were staying, too tired to flee once more. An old man sat calmly in his courtyard smoking a water-pipe, surrounded by a web of uprooted vines. In another courtyard an old woman, a machine gun on her lap, was having tea with a few soldiers. On the

ground there were traces of blood and bloody wads of cotton wool. All the time there was the acrid smoke of the phosphorus bombs rising from holes in the ground. The bombs had set houses alight and the smoke that envelops us scars the lungs. The number of damaged houses grew, . . . twenty . . . thirty-seven . . . fifty-two . . . sixty-five . . . . Through the big gaping holes in the wall of the last damaged house we visited, we saw the setting sun colour the sky and the Mediterranean a flaming orange.

'Seventy-six houses were hit today!' Abu Ahmed said, as he shut his notebook. 'But that's only the houses. Seven people are injured, one very badly, while many people have slight injuries. People have time to retreat to the shelters when there is shelling, shells cause mainly material damage. But, when the bombers come, there is never time to get down to them and then usually twenty, thirty, forty people are killed.

We missed the BBC news on the radio that night but listened to the Voice of America instead, in tense anticipation of a report of the Israeli attack on the Sour area and on the camps, how

thousands upon thousands of Palestinians were escaping north
. . . . But all we heard was that Palestinian 'terrorists' had been
firing at the kibbutz of Metullah in Northern Israel. One person
was dead and several were injured. The inhabitants had had to
retire to the shelters. Israel was considering the possibility of
bombing civilian targets in Lebanon in retaliation . . . . *Possibly
beginning to bomb!* Could it be true that news could be reported
in this way throughout the world? Not a word said about the fact
that Israel has *already* bombed civilian targets, women and
children and people's homes . . . that Palestinians in the camps had
been sleeping in shelters for weeks . . . . When we told Abu Ahmed
about the report, he laughed briefly in his quiet manner and gave
a slight shrug, as people do when they know that they are
subjected to unfair treatment.

> What do you expect? I'm not surprised, we're used to this.
> The world is always told about every little thing that the
> Palestinians do against the Israelis — every operation, every
> time we fire across the border. The Zionists have such great
> power to spread their propaganda. They claim that they
> bomb the Palestinian camps in self-defence. The Israelis
> have the latest, most modern weapons, they have everything,
> bombers, gunboats, rockets . . . . What have we got? Machine
> guns, light artillery, anti aircraft defence . . . we haven't
> got a chance even to counter an attack! But we are called
> terrorists!

In the evening the whole camp seemed deserted. Seventy per
cent of the population, some 11,000 people, had left Rashidiyeh.
Our footsteps echoed in the pitch black alleys as we walked home
with Abu Ahmed. A man's deep voice suddenly addressed us in
the dark.
   '*Miin?*' — Who's there?
   '*Aiwa! Aiwa!*' — It's okay, Abu Ahmed replies quietly. An older
man dressed in a *gallabiya* and a*koffiya* and carrying a machine
gun was caught in the beam of our torch. He was the guard. During our
our short walk home, this was repeated several times.
   Later that evening we were sitting around a gas ring on the floor
in Um Ali's house. The electricity had gone out all over Southern
Lebanon. Um Ali's family was one of the few which had stayed
in the camp. 'We're staying,' the oldest son, Ali, said. Abu Ali
nodded in agreement. 'It's not a good thing if everyone leaves.

We've got everything here. Our home, our work, the school . . . .'
The children were half asleep each on top of the other under
blankets on the floor. Um Ali looked at them. 'The children want
to leave,' she said. 'They are terrified! I suppose I'll have to take
them to Beirut tomorrow. They know very well what they are
doing, the Zionists. Haddad fires at us too, the cad, they go hand
in hand to try to finish us off. They want to empty Southern
Lebanon so that they can invade after that!'

The following morning we were awakened by the silence. A
ghostly silence. No prayer calls were heard at daybreak, no voices
or screams of children, no radios. But the hush of the sea seemed
louder. The crowing of a lonely cock resounded through the air.
Nobody washed up at the water-conduit, no taxis collected
commuters for Sour, no children went to school. Abu Nimmer's
shop was locked. The water in the puddles lay smooth and still.
But some old people were still to be seen walking slowly along the

114

alleys. A family appeared with suitcases and a transistor radio, they sat down by the water-conduit, waiting for a taxi. A bent old man with a bundle on his shoulder, his grandson at his heels, began his long journey to Sour. Later that morning the soldiers began to mend the electricity supply. Abu Ali played badminton in the alley. But everything was done in a quiet and subdued manner.

Um Ali approached us beaming, her arms extended. 'Palestinians have achieved three operations inside Israel today! We're paying them back!' she said, hugging us both.

17. Without The Women The Revolution Has No Future

We left Rashidiyeh to return to Beirut. Our time in Lebanon was almost at an end. One of the last people we met before leaving was Um Leila. She was sitting alone in a room at the Palestine Research Centre with its three desks and metal book shelves. Through the windows we saw the many rooftops of Beirut and the mountains to the north beyond the right-wing stronghold of Jounieh. It was only natural that we should discuss the bombings of Southern Lebanon. 'It's awful,' she said, her voice echoing in the bare room. 'And it will get worse. The tension is mounting all the time.' Um Leila looked dejected when we told her what had happened in the camps around Sour. She put her hands on the glass top of the desk.

Well, you can't cry over each tragedy that happens . . . . If we did, we'd never do anything else. We must always try to find some positive side . . . I'm glad you stayed long enough to see an Israeli attack. Now you've seen what the war does to us, what it means, how it forces our people to live. It's always difficult to explain this to foreigners who have never experienced anything similar . . . .

I was pregnant when the war started. My daughter was only four months old when the Syrians came and bombed our camp here in Beirut. I didn't see her for two months! I came home at one in the morning and left at about 6 a.m. on those few occasions when I did come home. She didn't even recognize me when I saw her again! Now, I ask myself . . . how *could* I have left my daughter for two months? Now, I can't understand it. But in such times it becomes natural. The collective task is put before children, husband . . . before everything! On the occasions when I went home and they returned to the camps on the following days, I saw how people waited for me in the shelters, waited for me to bring them news, reports . . . of course, that sort of thing has to come before one's family! During bomb attacks, during war, all one's everyday problems disappear . . . all the normal values in life disappear completely! Everything changes . . . .

We thought of Mouna and her work in Rashidiyeh, how all the things built up by her and by the other activists in the Women's Association were being torn down by the Israeli bombs; and how the women with renewed effort start again, only to find their work ruined once more when the Israelis return. Mouna, the messenger, running alone through the alleys while shells fell around her, Mouna hurrying back to the shelter to report events.

'Mouna is highly esteemed, did you notice that? Her job is different, the men couldn't do it, and that's why they listen to her. A woman does not have to fight at the front to be respected!'

We have to leave. Um Leila gets up from behind the desk shakes hands with us and says:

One final thing, one thing you must mention in your book. Write that in spite of all the obstacles, in spite of war and death, in spite of the opposition from the men, the Palestinian women will participate in the liberation struggle. It is very important! It means that they believe in the Revolution and will teach their children to believe in it. Without the women the Revolution would be without a future. Every day people are killed amongst us, every day produces a martyr. If people don't understand the situation we live, they won't understand the pain that makes mothers wish, more than anything else, for their sons to become commandos!

18. Epilogue

Two and a half years have elapsed since we huddled together with Mouna's family in the bomb shelter as Israeli shells pounded Rashidiyeh. The shelling in January 1979 marked the beginning of an eight-month long Israeli offensive in Southern Lebanon. The offensive reached its peak that summer when Israel shelled the area for 113 consecutive days. Israel did not direct its fire only against the Palestinian refugee camps. Lebanese towns and villages were also shelled. More than 200,000 Palestinian and Lebanese civilians had to flee north to the crowded slum districts and refugee camps in Beirut and Sidon. Three hundred people lost their lives and more than 7,000 homes were destroyed.

Only half of Rashidiyeh's population returned after the offensive. Fearing new rounds of shelling, the other half remained in the north. Their fears were well-founded. Since the end of 1979, Southern Lebanon has only enjoyed one brief period of relative calm.

Rashidiyeh has been shelled regularly, sometimes daily and for months on end. The 8,000 refugees who still live there spend much of their time in the camp's bomb shelters. They sleep there almost every night. The once lively camp streets are now quiet and empty. Practically every other house in the camp has been destroyed or damaged. Rashidiyeh's school has received a large number of direct hits. And as if the constant threat of new Israeli shellings is not enough, the camp also has to cope with the hordes of rats, wild cats and dogs who have moved into the abandoned houses.

Very little of this is ever reported in the Western press. At best, one may find a brief news item in the morning paper about how Israeli forces have attacked 'Palestinian terrorist bases in the Tyre district', Israel's term for Rashidiyeh and the other refugee

120

camps there. It seems that more spectacular forms of suffering are required in order to create headlines here in the West.

The most recent reminder of this was Israel's devastating air raid on Beirut on 17 July 1981. In less than 45 minutes, Israeli bombs demolished several city blocks, killing 300 people and seriously wounding a further 800.

The raid preceded yet another major Israeli offensive in Lebanon. The Damour, Sidon, Nabatiya and Tyre areas were bombed and shelled for eight days as Israeli forces systematically destroyed the bridges crossing the Litani River. As Southern Lebanon was cut off from the rest of the country, fears rose that Israel was planning once again to invade the area. When incidents were reported even along the Israeli-Syrian ceasefire line, a flurry of Big Power diplomatic activity finally led to a new fragile truce. Once again, the world could lean back in relief. Once again, a fifth Middle East War had been temporarily avoided.

But there is no relief in sight for Mouna and her neighbours in Rashidiyeh. Israeli gunboats continue to prowl along the coast, Israeli planes still fly over the camp and the risk from sudden shelling is always there.

Ingela Bendt and Jim Downing
Stockholm
1981.

19. Palestine's History: A Chronology

Palestine is situated in the so-called Fertile Crescent, an area extending over today's Iraq, Syria, Lebanon and Israel. Due to its abundance of fertile land and its geographically important position as a communication link between Africa and Asia, Palestine has been conquered some thirty times in its 5,000 year history.

The people of Canaan were a nomadic tribe who came to Palestine from the desert several thousand years before Christ, and were probably the first people to inhabit the area. They called their country 'Canaan'. The word 'Palestine' was coined by the Greeks and means 'the country of the Philistines', a people who conquered the coastal area of Canaan around 1400 BC. They called their country 'Philistia'. The Arabic name for Palestine is ,Philestin'. Palestine came under Arab rule and, like Jordan and Lebanon comprised part of Great Syria. Palestine was rechristened 'Istael' in 1948 when immigrating European Jews proclaimed their own state there.

2800 BC	Egyptian Pharaohs invade Canaan. Thousands of her inhabitants are taken to Egypt as slaves.
1850 BC	Lack of food makes the Hebrews leave their home town of Ur (in today's Iraq) and emigrate to Canaan. Their leader is Abraham. The Hebrews have *one* god only. Their religion is Judaism.
1400 BC	Arameans and Philistines immigrate to Canaan. The various tribes make war on another for centuries.
1004 BC	The Hebrews secure political control of most of Canaan under their kings David and Solomon. Their kingdom is called Israel. Their capital is Jerusalem.
930 BC	Barely 70 years after its formation, the Hebrew kingdom is divided into two — Judaea and Samaria — which are later conquered successively by

Babylonians, Persians, Greeks and finally Romans.

70 AD   After a Jewish rebellion in the Roman province of Palestine, the Romans destroy Jerusalem and forbid the Jews to enter. The Jews are taken captive and sent off to Rome, others emigrate to different parts of Europe and North Africa. Some of them stay in Palestine and other parts of the Middle East.

630 AD   An army led by the prophet Mohammed, the founder of Islam, conquers the city of Mecca on the Arabian peninsula, today's Saudi Arabia. The Arabs are converted to Islam and march out to invade the rest of the world.

636 AD   The Arabs conquer the rest of the Middle East and march on to Turkey and North Africa. Palestine becomes Arabic. The Koran is compiled.

1099 AD   European Crusaders occupy Palestine but are driven out by the Arabs 100 years later.

1516   The Ottomans from Turkey conquer the whole of the Middle East, including Palestine. The Ottomans control the Middle East for 400 years.

19th Century   Jews are persecuted in Europe. Small groups of European Jews begin to emigrate to Palestine where they assimilate with the Arab population and find a sanctuary to practise their religion. As European colonialism conquers almost the entire world, Zionism is created, a political movement claiming that all Jews have an *exclusive* Biblical right to Palestine.

At the same time, the Ottoman rule of Palestine and the Middle East is getting weaker. A French-British consortium builds the Suez Canal through Egypt. The Canal is opened in 1869. It becomes an important shortcut to French and British colonies, important enough for England to incorporate Egypt in the Empire in 1882. The Suez Canal and the important strategic position of the Middle East makes the area indispensable to the colonialists.

In 1896 Theodor Herzl, one of the founders of Zionism, writes his book, *The Jewish State*, where he advocates the formation of a Jewish state in Palestine. The following year the Zionist movement holds its first congress in Basle, Switzerland. The

Zionists start to organize large-scale emigration of Jews to Palestine.

1908   The first oil in the Middle East is found by Britons in Iran.

1914-16   The First World War breaks out. The Ottomans in Turkey anxiously watch the increased influence of Britain and France in the Middle East and ally themselves with Germany.

The Zionists turn to Britain and suggest that it should support the Jewish immigration to Palestine in exchange for the promise that a future Jewish state would take care of British interests in the Suez Canal.

At the same time Britain promises the Arabs independence if they rise against the Ottomans. The Arabs start a rebellion.

In the meantime, Britain and France meet secretly and plan a division of the Middle East in anticipation of their defeating the Ottomans.

1917   *The Balfour Declaration* 2 November: The British Foreign Secretary, Lord Balfour, expresses the support of the British Government for the formation of 'a national home for Jews in Palestine'. The Arabs protest. Britain placates them by promising that the Jewish immigration will be handled in a way that will not harm the political and economic interests of the Palestinians. 2 November has become a day of national mourning for the Palestinians.

1918   The Arabs liberate Damascus from Ottoman rule, but in spite of earlier promises of Arab independence, Britain takes over control of Damascus a month later.

Britain, France and the US win the First World War.

1920-39   The League of Nations is formed with an obvious European majority among member states. The League gives France a mandate over Syria, whilst Britain is given Iraq, Jordan and Palestine. 'Mandate' simply means that Britain and France administer these areas as *de facto* colonies.

With the approval of the British, the Zionists start a massive emigration of European Jews to Palestine. Between 1919 and 1936, Palestine's Jewish population grows from 58,000 to 348,000. In the same period the Arab population of Palestine grows from

642,000 to 978,000. The Zionists form the Jewish National Fund to buy up land in Palestine but manage to increase their share of the land by only 5.6%.

The Palestinians object to the mounting Zionist immigration, but Britain does not react. Palestine proclaims a national strike in 1936 to protest Zionist immigration. The strike soon turns into an armed rebellion against the British. Together with the Zionists, the British put down the rebellion in 1939.

1939-45   The Second World War breaks out. In Palestine the British make a U-turn and suddenly try to limit Zionist immigration in order to stop the Arabs supporting Germany. The Zionists organize illegal immigration and openly oppose the British.

In Europe Hitler begins the extermination of the Jews. Six million Jews are murdered before Nazi Germany is defeated. More than 200,000 Jews manage to emigrate to Palestine under the Zionist programme.

The UN is formed.

Syria, Lebanon and Jordan become independent, but *not* Palestine.

1946   Violent clashes between Zionists and Palestinians. Britain loses control of the situation and leaves the responsibility of Palestine with the UN.

1947   The UN decides to divide Palestine into a Jewish and and an Arab state. The Palestinians who do not want to see their country divided reject the partition plan. The Zionists prepare for the introduction of partition and begin a terrorist campaign against the Palestinians to make them flee.

1948   British troops leave Palestine. Zionists proclaim the Jewish State of Israel. The Arab states send in armies against the new state. 800,000 Palestinians flee before the advancing Israeli troops. The Arab armies are forced to retreat but manage to stop the Israeli invasion of the West Bank of the Jordan and Gaza.

Jordan annexes the West Bank.

1949   Israel is accepted as a member state of the UN. At the same time, the UN instructs Israel to let the Palestinians return but Israel refuses. The Palestinians end up in refugee camps run by the UN in Jordan,

Lebanon, Syria and Gaza. The Palestinians do not build up any resistance movement but become apathetic, waiting for the Arab armies to liberate Palestine.

1956   Egypt nationalizes the Suez Canal. Israel, Britain and France invade Egypt. The Soviet Union threatens to bomb Paris and London. The US force the invaders to retire.

A group of Palestinian students — one of them Yasser Arafat — decide to take the matter into their own hands and form a Palestinian resistance movement — Fatah.

1964   The Arab states form the PLO (Palestine Liberation Organization). Fatah stays outside because they think the PLO is too much under the incluence of the Arab states.

1965   1 January: Fatah stages its first guerrilla operation inside Israel.

1967   *The June War:* In six days Israel trebles her territory by occupying the Sinai peninsula in Egypt, the Golan Heights in Syria, the West Bank and Gaza. Now all of Palestine is occupied by the Zionists. 416,000 new refugees from the West Bank and Gaza flee to Jordan, Egypt and Syria. The Arab armies are vanquished. The super-powers — the US and the USSR — start a diplomatic offensive to get the Arab states to recognize Israel in return for Israel giving back the occupied areas. *Not a word is mentioned about the national rights of the Palestinians.*

1968-69   The military void after the defeat of the Arab armies in the June War is soon filled by Fatah. Several other commando groups, such as the Popular Front and the Democratic Front, are formed. In 1969 the commando groups take over the PLO and the Fatah leader Yasser Arafat is elected the PLO Chairman.

Guerrilla bases are set up in Jordan but also in Lebanon where a reluctant Government gives the PLO the right to carry out actions against Israel from Lebanese territory.

The PLO takes over the control of refugee camps in Lebanon and Jordan.

1971   *Black September:* The numerous guerrilla operations of the PLO from Jordan, Israel's revenge actions against guerrilla bases and Jordanian villages, and the increasing military strength of the PLO lead to a direct confrontation between the liberation movement and King Hussein of Jordan. After many battles, Hussein's army manages to drive the liberation movement out of Jordan in September 1971 after a massacre of thousands of Palestinians. The PLO move their headquarters from Jordan to Lebanon.

Egypt's President Nasser dies. Sadat takes over.

1973   *The October War:* The Middle East peace initiative of the great powers peters out because Israel refuses to compromise. To break the deadlock, Egypt and Syria start an offensive against Israel's forces in Sinai and Golan. Israel is forced to retreat slightly in both areas. New peace negotiations start.

1974   The PLO Chairman Yasser Arafat addressed the UN General Assembly. For the first time in the history of the UN, the leader of a liberation movement is allowed to speak. A majority of the countries of the world — 105 states — recognize the PLO as the sole legitimate representative of the Palestinian people. At the same time, the UN acknowledges the Palestinians' *right to a home country of their own.*

1975   The numerous guerrilla operations from Southern Lebanon prompt Israel to start intensive bombing campaigns of the Palestinian refugee camps in the area. They also attack Lebanese villages to force the population to flee. Zionists maintain that Southern Lebanon also belongs to the Jewish state.

Civil war breaks out in Lebanon. The Lebanese right wing attacks Palestinian refugee camps in the Beirut area and the PLO is drawn into fighting on the side of the Lebanese left wing.

The UN condemns Zionism as a form of racism.

Egypt under Sadat and Israel sign an agreement, at the prompting of the US, Israeli withdrawal from Sinai.

1976   Syria enters the Lebanese Civil War on the side of the right wing to end the conflict.

1977   Egypt's President, Anwar Sadat, travels to Jerusalem to start serious peace negotiations. His visit is condemned by the Arab League, in particular by the PLO.

1978 Israel invades Southern Lebanon in March but is
     forced to retreat.

     A preliminary peace treaty is signed by Israel and
     Egypt at Camp David in the U.S.

1979 A final peace treaty is signed between Israel and
     Egypt whilst the Israeli air force is bombing
     Palestinian refugee camps in Lebanon.

     Lebanese right-wing forces supported by Israel
     proclaim their own state in parts of South Lebanon.

1980 War breaks out between Iran and Iraq.

1981 Israeli bombers attack and destroy a nuclear reactor
     in Baghdad, Iraq.

     300 people are killed and 800 are wounded in an
     Israeli air raid against Beirut. Israeli forces systematic-
     ally destroy the bridges across the Litani River,
     leading to new fears of an Israeli invasion of Southern
     Lebanon.

20. How Many Palestinians?

Because the Palestinians have been scattered all over the world, it is impossible to give an exact figure of their numbers. Some Palestinians have become citizens of the country they now inhabit. Others have not registered as camp refugees with the UN. During the last fourteen years of standstill and unrest, many Palestinians have died or been born without having been registered anywhere. The following figures are based partly on the calculations of the PLO and partly on statistics from Israel and the UN in 1975. All figures are approximate and probably much higher today.

Israel (1967 borders)	520,000
West Bank and Gaza	1,100,000
Jordan	960,000
Lebanon	260,000
Syria	170,000
Egypt	35,000
Kuwait	170,000
Libya	7,000
Saudi Arabia	25,000
Iraq	15,000
United Arab Emirates	18,000
The US, Latin America and Europe	165,000
Total No. of Palestinians	*3,445,000*

Of these, according to the UN, 641,000 live in 59 refugee camps in Lebanon, Syria, Jordan, the West Bank and Gaza.

OTHER TITLES FROM LAWRENCE HILL & Co.

Inger Holt-Seeland
Women of Cuba
Hb and Pb

Marta Harnecker
Cuba: Dictatorship or Democracy?
Hb and Pb

A.W. Singham (ed)
The Non-Aligned Movement in World Politics
Pb

Roderick Stewart
The Mind of Norman Bethune
Hb

Langston Hughes
Good Morning Revolution
Uncollected Writings of Social Protest
Pb

Claudia Zaslavsky
Africa Counts
Number and Pattern in African Culture
Pb

Mohamed El-Khawas and Barry Cohen
The Kissinger Study of Southern Africa
National Security Study Memorandum 39 (Secret)
Pb

Lawrence Hill titles cover American Studies, Europe, Politics,
Literature, and Africa.

**You can order Lawrence Hill titles from Lawrence Hill & Co.,
520 Riverside Avenue, Westport, Conn. 06880, USA, or from
Zed Press, 57 Caledonian Road, London, N1 9DN, UK.**

OTHER BOOKS AVAILABLE FROM ZED PRESS

On the Middle East

Kamal Joumblatt
I Speak for Lebanon
Hb and Pb

Ghali Shoukri
Egypt: Portrait of a President
Sadat's Road to Jerusalem
Hb and Pb

B. Berberoglu
Turkey in Crisis
From State Capitalism to Neo-Colonialism
Hb and Pb

Samir Amin
The Arab Economy Today
Hb

Jan Metzger, Martin Orth and Christian Sterzing
This Land is Our Land
The West Bank Under Israell Occupation
Hb and Pb

Ingela Bendt and Jim Downing
We Shall Return
Women of Palestine
Hb and Pb

Juliette Minces
The House of Obedience
Women in Arab Society
Hb and Pb

Mina Modares and Azar Tabari
In the Shadow of Islam
The Women's Movement in Iran
Hb and Pb

Nawal el Saadawi
The Hidden Face of Eve
Women in the Arab World
Hb and Pb

Samir Amin
The Arab Nation
Nationalism and Class Struggles
Hb and Pb

Gerard Chaliand (Ed.)
People Without A Country
The Kurds and Kurdistan
Hb and Pb

Bizhan Jazani
Capitalism and Revolution in Iran
Hb and Pb

Terisa Turner and Petter Nore (Eds.)
Oil and Class Struggle
Hb and Pb

Maxime Rodinson
Marxism and the Muslim World
Hb and Pb

Rosemary Sayigh
Palestinians: From Peasants to Revolutionaries
Hb and Pb

People's Press
Our Roots Are Still Alive
Pb

Zed press titles cover Africa, Asia, Latin America and the Middle East, as well as general issues affecting the Third World's relations with the rest of the world. Our Series embrace: Imperialism, Women, Political Economy, History, Labour, Voices of Struggle, Human Rights and other areas pertinent to the Third World.

You can order Zed titles direct from Zed Press, 57 Caledonian Road, London, N1 9DN, U.K.